Thanks for all the
Support & advice! means
a lot! I hope we keep
in touch throughout the years!
Enjoy the read and thanks
for everything! -

TO: Bruce

Thanks for all the support & advice! means a lot! I hope we keep in touch throughout the years!

Enjoy the read and thanks for everything! -

David Bagga

The Walk-On

David Bagga

authorHOUSE®

AuthorHouse™
1663 Liberty Drive
Bloomington, IN 47403
www.authorhouse.com
Phone: 1-800-839-8640

First published by AuthorHouse   12/17/2010

ISBN: 978-1-4490-4179-3 (e)
ISBN: 978-1-4490-3772-7 (sc)
ISBN: 978-1-4490-3773-4 (hc)

Library of Congress Control Number: 2009910809

Printed in the United States of America

This book is printed on acid-free paper.

Certain stock imagery © *Thinkstock.*

To Coach Olson ...

Coach Olson if it wasn't for you I wouldn't have been able to have the experience of a lifetime. I can't tell you how much you mean to me as a Coach, mentor and friend, thank you so much for everything.

"People of Mediocre ability sometimes achieve outstanding success because they don't know when to quit. Most men succeed because they are defined to". - George Allen

Acknowledgment

Dear Friends, Fans, and supporters of the program,

Hey everyone, I'm writing this book to share my experience about what it was like walking on to the basketball team for four years and sharing all the experiences I had while playing here. First of all let me just say a few things on my behalf, my time at the University of Arizona was unbelievable and it was something I'll always remember for the rest of my life. I consider myself fortunate to be able to play at such a prestigious program for 4 years. I also feel fortunate enough to play for a hall of fame coach as well. I know I only had Coach Olson for 2 years but he taught me so much and gave me so many opportunities on and off the court. I wish him nothing but the best and I can't thank him enough for everything he did for me. To give you guys an idea of what type of guy Coach Olson was, read this.

Every practice we would stretch out as a team and then have a few minutes to loosen up on our own while our coaches would go over the practice schedule and while we were stretching out Coach Olson would make his way around the court and talk to us for a quick minute or so, sometimes guys were getting stretched by our strength coach or our trainer Justin and we usually had our own little areas where we loosened ourselves up. My area was the back corner near the basket closest to our bench, every practice I stretched out there and every other Practice Coach Olson would come and talk to me and ask me how everything was going. Whether it was my classes or my family or just him checking in with me, he always took the time to do that.

That by itself just goes to show people what type of person Lute Olson is; see I was a "walk-on" but not once did he ever treat me like a walk-on. If the truth be known he treated me like I was an all-American even though I never really played until the end of the game when we were up by a pretty good amount. When I think about my experience with Coach Olson that always sticks out in my mind because he genuinely cared about all of us whether we started and played forty minutes a game or forty seconds a game, whether we were the all Americans going to the NBA or we were on the bench waiving a towel around and pushing other players in practice to get better.

My freshman year at Arizona was great, we had a few more losses than we had hoped for but we wound up making the tournament and losing to Villanova in the 2nd round of the tournament. It was about three weeks later I went into Coach Olson's office as we had our exit meetings for the season and I had told him that I had been journaling every night during the season and I had thought about writing a book about my experience as a walk-on.

My reasoning for doing this was because I wanted to give people a different view, a view that nobody had really ever seen before and that was the view from the bench. I promised him that I would never say a down word about the program because I didn't get a raw deal in terms of playing time or anything like that. I was a walk-on and I relished every moment of it. But I am being truthful with everything that has been written in here, and you'll see that when you read this.

Call me crazy but there was always something intriguing about cheering my ass off for four years on that bench and going crazy when my teammates or I did something spectacular in a game. I got a lot of joy watching them in games because I knew I had the chance to push them everyday in practice and it made me feel pretty good. But there was always more to it than just basketball, the academic side of walking on, the social aspect, and the emotional and psychological part as well. Of course there were those days when I thought I wasn't going to make it and I couldn't do it.

Then there were the days when I thought I was a good enough player to start for this team. All of that was a big part of the process of being a walk-on and the ups and downs I experienced everyday. Most of the times were great experiences because this was what I wanted and I soaked up as much as I could for four years. Even if something was bad I did the most of it to make it a good situation. In the back of my mind I knew that it was going to be a grind playing and being a student so I had to do as much as I can to make it the best experience.

In my opinion there was no greater feeling than being able to compete on a daily basis with my teammates and build friendships with them while doing so. All in all this experience was a phenomenal one and reflecting back on everything I was glad I embarked on the journey.

I know a lot of fans thought the years of 2005-2009 of Arizona basketball were somewhat rocky; but if you asked me I wouldn't have changed the way the seasons went. The way we played and the way we battled spoke highly about our character as a team; and we did make that sweet sixteen run my senior year which is something a lot of people will remember for a long time. Anyway this book came from my heart and I hope you guys enjoy reading this story; Bear Down.

Chapter 1

WHEN I HEARD THE squeaking of the other shoes on the court I took a step back to see where I was at, as I heard the 9 other players talking on the court beside me I knew the atmosphere was so different, so unique, so incredible. I took a look around me and realized that I had been living out an experience of a lifetime, wearing a jersey that said ARIZONA on the front and engraved on the back of the jersey was BAGGA with a big #11 underneath my name. I didn't have time to reminisce about all this stuff because I had just checked into our first home game against Virginia and seconds later I would come off of a screen to score my first collegiate basket. There were so many emotions I was feeling after I scored. My dream had become an unlikely reality and suddenly I found myself caught up in the moment. The arena was so loud I couldn't hear myself think; all I could do was smile and soak up the experience and think about how many more there were to come.

A journey is defined as a passage or progress from one stage of life to the next. Opportunity is defined as a chance for progress or advancement. In life when we have opportunities we must grab them by the neck to get an experience that is much wanted. In my life I have had many opportunities come before me that I have either turned down, ran away from, or just did not care about. But this opportunity was unlike any other opportunity that had ever crossed my path. This is my story, my journey, my opportunity, my experience that changed my life...We have all heard the old saying "Be the best you can be" and that applies to virtually everything in life, from language to lay-ups, science to slam dunks, history to

1

hoops… you guys get the idea. To be the best at something, whatever it is in life, we have to learn to make sacrifices, which I definitely learned to do.

Like every other story, there is a beginning. It was my dream to play college basketball. Across the country there were hundreds of thousands of kids that could do way more things than I could. How I got to be a division one basketball player is really a story within a story. In a way, my story is your story, surrounded around a mediocre bubble filled with highs, lows, and everything else in-between.

In high school I always thought I should've received playing time for what I did in practice, I was matched up with starters and guys who were fortunate enough to earn scholarships to respective schools. I used to hear my teammates in high school talking about how proud their families were of them when they signed their name on that dotted line, meaning they had a place to go play basketball for the next season.

I can only describe my experience as a high school basketball player with one word: Ironic. I was a 3rd string player which meant I didn't play very much. Every time we had a game I got used to seeing those 3 letters next to my name: DNP which stands for did not play. My high school teammates were arrogant, the guys that started had an ego the size of Texas and a swagger about them like everything they did was picture perfect.

Of course I couldn't have that ego, because I was that guy on the bench waiting and wishing for an opportunity to show my teammates, peers, and family that I belonged out there too. But reality hit me that practice was my time to ultimately shine in front of people.

I was one of those guys that were lost, I went to a big time high school to make a name for myself and instead I found a bench for myself to sit on game after game of every season. I had heard it my whole life leading up to my high school graduation: "That kid that has potential but is lazy or doesn't have the grades or doesn't work as hard as the other guys". I never understood it because in my mind all I needed was an opportunity to show people what I could do.

During my final semester in high school I couldn't let a day go by without talking to my parents about anything, specifically college. My parents used to harp that going to college and getting a degree was important because it opened up so many doors that people without degrees wouldn't have access to. I just wanted to go to college to play basketball, I didn't care where, what level, or who my teammates were, I just wanted to go play so that one day in my life I could look back and say "I did it".

Every night before I went to bed the last thing I told myself was that there was someone out there willing to give me a chance. As unrealistic as it seemed, there was someone listening to me those nights.

I was struggling so much to even think about anything else, grades, girls, a social life, all because of how much playing college basketball meant to me. I knew I had to take a risk and even if I failed and wound up not getting accepted into a college I could look back and say I gave it a shot. I started filling out college applications left and right, any place anybody could think of I was the first person to inquire online or through the phone thinking how great it would be if one coach gave me the time of day.

Very rarely did I call the admissions offices because my main goal was to get in close with coaching staffs, the guys who would make the final decisions about letting me into a university. I figured if I got in close with them they could vouch for me on my behalf with the people who worked in admissions. After practice, I'd usually go into our library for an hour so and look up all the mid-major colleges across the country. I tried to do as much research as I could and hone in on rosters, coaches, enrollment and any other important information so I could have a talking point when I tried to pitch myself to coaches.

I developed an elevator speech but luckily these coaches couldn't see me and see my face when I made the calls out to them every other day. I started this whole process out by calling schools on the other side of the country that nobody had ever heard of before. Schools like Austin Pea University and Middle Tennessee State University. I figured if I had a chance of walking on it would more than likely be with mediocre schools like these.

Surprisingly some of the coaches actually picked up their phones and answered. The first thing I did was hang up the phone and then try calling again. Nerves began to take over my mind and my body, every time I made one of these calls to a coach I used to look at myself in the mirror for a split second and ask "Why?" Why was I doing this? Any 18 year old who uses common sense knows that the prototypical path would've been attending a community college for a 2 years and then getting recruited. But I decided to take a risk because of how I was brought up and what I believed in.

When I was fortunate enough to connect with coaches over the phone they usually didn't know who I was, why I was calling, and sometimes why I was wasting their time. Only when I mentioned the name of my high school, Mater Dei, the coaches began to take a percent of interest in me. "Do you have a highlight tape?" The different coaches would ask. "No", I would tell them in an awkward, embarrassed voice. I tried to avoid that question every time and the more coaches I called the worse it got.

"Why should we let you walk-on to our program?" One coach asked. "I can bring a lot to the table" I said enthusiastically, knowing they couldn't get a read on me. Usually after I said that there was a pause on the other end of the phone for a few seconds before a coach would bring me back down to earth and let me know how many kids were vying for spots on a team.

That was the beauty of this whole risk-taking experiment to try and go to college and play basketball. I felt like a person without a library card trying to get into the library and being asked all these different questions about why I should have admission. Days became weeks and weeks became months and I had no clue if I was even going to college. Our high school team was making a run towards a city championship and like some of the other guys who didn't play; I was along for the ride hoping to hear my number called.

I used to get embarrassed when my high school coach would throw me in there for a minute or so at the end of the games to kill time and make it look like he was doing his good deed to society by making me look like a charity case. I would look different directions and see fans quietly exiting because they already knew the outcome of the game. The college coaches and scouts that eagerly showed up at the beginning would find their way out through the back door and yet somehow a part of me thought they would wait to check out what I could do.

As we progressed deeper into the high school playoffs, I knew the clock was ticking faster and faster. Secretly I was still applying to schools left and right and hoping for my dream to become a reality. I used to see some of my teammates go home with stacks and stacks of letters everyday from schools like Duke, North Carolina, Villanova, UCLA, etc. I would've killed for something like that to happen to me. I used to think if I could re-wind time and do it all over again I would've gone to a smaller high school so I would've been a big fish in a small pond as oppose to being a little fish still learning how to swim. I kept calling universities and coaches from around the country and received similar responses, but no response was as brutal as the first response that I received.

So as I moved on to schools close to home, I decided that I wanted to stay on the west-coast for different reasons like weather, atmosphere, and the fact that most of the universities are relatively close to my home, which is nice because I'm not on the other side of the country away from my family and friends. As I narrowed down my choices I looked at all the different conferences in which collegiate teams compete in and the conference that I thought I would fit into would be the Pacific ten conference or also known as the "PAC 10" because they have great schools from top to bottom and great tradition as well. I did not apply to certain schools for personal reasons and I did not want to set myself up for something that would not happen.

So I was down to my final six schools in the running; Washington, WSU, Oregon, OSU, Arizona State, and University of Arizona. When I filled out my applications, I thought to myself that this was my last chance to make something happen. Ironically I received the letters denying me acceptance into Washington State, Oregon, and Oregon State on the same day. So I knew that those three were out of the running. So it was down to Washington, Arizona State, and University of Arizona. Three more weeks went by and I did not get accepted into Washington and I never heard back from Arizona State.

My parents often told me that with my grades and my attitude I had a long shot to get into a school, especially to play basketball. My dad would carefully remind me that coaches recruit the kids who receive playing time, not the kids with mediocre grades and sub-par skills.

I used to think to myself that if one of these schools called me up sometime and responded to the messages I left, I wouldn't know what to do with myself.

When my mom was dropping me off at school one day, she saw me playing with this piece of paper that had a gentleman's name and number on it. The piece of paper that was folded in half read "Jack Murphy: UA Basketball" followed by his number. She kept asking me why I had the piece of paper and what I intended to do with it. "I want to try and talk to the University of Arizona" I told her, while looking out the window. "We've been through this too many times", she would say, pointing out that I wasn't a shoe in to go to any college.

As much as my parents believed in me, I don't think they even gave me a fair shot to get into a good school. It killed me inside that my two "biggest fans" harped on grades and nothing else, causing them to sound like a broken record. I got so distracted talking to her that I put the piece of paper down on the car mattress in-between my legs and I forgot to take it with me as I got out of her car and headed for class. I told my mom not to tell my dad what I was doing because I was so sick and tired of getting lectured by my parents each and every day.

I went to class and frantically I was searching for my piece of paper with that guy's number on it. I couldn't find it at all and little did I know my mom took action into her own hands. She called the number to the University of Arizona admissions department. I called my mom when she was at home and I asked her if she had checked the mail yet. She told me that she had not yet checked it but she will later on. Before she did that, she made a call to U of A to talk about my application and my transcripts and whether or not I had been accepted into the university or not.

After the talk about school and grades had settled down, she asked to be transferred to the basketball office. They transferred her and someone wound up picking up the phone. So here is my mom, talking to national Powerhouse University of Arizona on the other line and here I am still in school thinking about everything else and what's going to happen with me and my future.

She called me while I was at practice and said that she had "great news" for me when I come home. The car ride home was anything but quiet. "I talked to U of A today", she said. "About what?" I asked. "About you walking-on", she said with a huge smile on her face. She said she had talked to the recruiting coordinator named Jack Murphy and explained to him the details about where I play, my height, weight, and position. I still was in a little bit of disbelief because it sounded too good to be true. I remember the one thing she said on the way home which did not include her smiling. "He said he wanted to talk you about walking-on but only if you're serious about it", She said.

I thought that car-ride home was a big joke at first, until my mom gave me the paper with Jack Murphy's direct phone number on it. She told me that I was going to receive a phone call from him later that night and I didn't know what to think after that. When we got home I sprinted up to my room, closed the door, took as quick a shower as I could and then paced back and forth in my room waiting for this guy to call. I had my phone in my hand and it was vibrating. The number looked so foreign to me because of that 520 area code and I picked up the phone not knowing what to expect and the first thing I heard set the tone for the night. "Hello", I said in a scared, frail voice.

"This is Jack Murphy from the University of Arizona", he said. After a little while of me being shy and quiet and some of the awkward silence, I finally told him what my plan was". "I'd like to be a walk-on", I said. "Yeah that's what you're mom was saying earlier today when we spoke." He said. We wound up talking for about thirty minutes or so and after talking to him I now felt much more confident in myself. As we wrapped up the conversation, he told me that Coach Lute Olson was coming out to watch our practice the following week. I'm thinking to myself that this was my one and only chance to meet a hall of fame coach and talk to him about walking-on.

The last note that Murph made before we ended the conversation was to call him after I talked to coach to confirm with him that I met him and talked to him. After I got off the phone with him, I sat by myself for a little while and reflected on what had just happened. I later marked the date on my calendar and I noticed that the day that Coach Olson was coming out to our practice was on Valentines Day.

Chapter 2

WHEN VALENTINES DAY ROLLED around I had no clue how I was going to go about telling my high school coach that I had been talking to the University of Arizona about walking-on to their basketball team. My coach and I didn't get along that well and my mentality for him was simple, I never wanted to bother the guy, I just wanted to stay out of his way. I tried telling a few of the guys on the team that I had been talking to Arizona and naturally jealousy, anger and disbelief set in for no apparent reason. "Yeah right" some of the guys said. "What college coach in their right mind is going to look at a guy that doesn't play for more than a minute at the end of every game?" one guy said.

Guys laughed at me, some were laughing harder than I'd ever seen them laugh before. A few of the guys taunted me before we went to practice but some of them were set straight moments later as we walked into the gym. As I walked into the gym with my practice gear on and my ankles taped tight, I new that this opportunity was going to come once and only once and if I blew it, there would never be another opportunity like this.

As all my teammates made their way into they gym with our coaching staff, he followed right behind our head coach. There he was, Coach Lute Olson of the University of Arizona; I still couldn't believe he was here. He had such a presence about him when he entered the gym. He was the kind of guy that drew eyes to him wherever he went, not just because he was a hall of farmer but because of how graceful he was and the approach that he had.

Time kept passing by faster and faster and practice eventually started. As the practice kept passing, I noticed that my coach had introduced the majority of my teammates to Coach Olson except for me. I was having the practice of my life, hitting three point shots left and right and trying to be "the guy" that day, but it was almost like natural selection took over during practice and I was trying to delay the inevitable.

Every water break, bathroom break, or transition from one drill to the next I kept thinking "Okay, soon I'll get my turn to shake Coach Olson's hand", but it didn't happen. Slowly, I saw my opportunity come then go, and it was slipping away from me. As practice ended and Coach Olson left, I walked into the locker room with my head down and I felt like the world had just ended around me. My first reaction was to cry in front of everyone but I couldn't let them know I was hurting; I couldn't let them get the better of me.

As I continued to sit there quietly, one of my teammates came over to me and saw I was down and whispered something to me that I'd remember for the rest of my life. "Dave" he said. "Yeah", I said. "It's nothing personal but you're not even good enough to play at an NAIA school, I'm sorry you just needed to know that". All I could do was nod; I was at a loss for words. This guy was supposed to be my teammate and he had the nerve to say that.

When I was on the way home from school with my mom the car ride was pretty quiet. I looked out the window and felt desperate. That night when I called up Jack Murphy I didn't know how I was going to tell him that I didn't get to meet Coach Olson and talk to him about my plan. The first time I called there was no answer. The second time there was also no answer. The third time I called him and he picked up. "I didn't get to meet him", I said. "You didn't?" Murph said.

I felt like there was no point to talking to him anymore because it seemed like this was a long-shot which it was and I kept thinking to myself over and over again that he was going to let me down easy. All of a sudden he told me something. "We talked about it today with Coach", Murph said. "He said that you can walk-on". I'm thinking to myself, "Is this really happening right now or am I dreaming?" Sure enough this was real, not a dream, not a mirage, and not a lie, this was real. I was in so much shock I didn't know what to say, think, or do. "Are you serious?" I said. "Yeah, I am", He said.

The whole time I was talking to him I had this huge, giddy smile on my face, almost like the smile people have when they win a big prize in a contest. The smile was permanent for the next several days because of the news that I had just heard, but I knew that I couldn't tell anyone because this was something that I wanted to cherish for a while before I made it public to people. I later thanked him and we ended the conversation and my mom was right there next to me hugging me while I was on the phone. Pure jubilation had set in and I could only imagine what the next 4 years would entail.

My whole attitude towards high school basketball was different since I had been accepted into Arizona. I could've cared less if we won lost or even forfeited games. I was ready to begin the next chapter of my life as an Arizona Wildcat. The only thing that became alarming was the fact that a few weeks after I received the confirmation of being able to walk-onto the team, I had still not received my acceptance letter into the school.

Our team made it all the way to the state championship game and I had absolutely nothing to do with us getting there. I could accept that because in the back of my mind I knew I was off to something bigger and better and I was leaving behind something that was negative in a sense. If the truth be told, outside of a few of my high school teammates I was around a group of guys that didn't care about anyone else but themselves and I had a coach that played favorites and left some of us out to dry.

We wound up losing that game by 19 points and getting embarrassed. The locker room was full of crying teenagers who felt like we didn't accomplish what we had set out to do. I was one of the few guys in there not crying. I was just excited to get home and talk with my parents about college.

As we arrived back home in Orange County, my dad was waiting there and ready to take me home. The car ride home was quieter simply for the fact because I thought that my senior season was a waste. We didn't win a state championship and I was a third string player who didn't play at all and still didn't know where he was going to college at. I'll always remember the one thing that my dad told me as we were on our way home. "When one door closes, another door opens", he said. I really wasn't paying attention until I got home and opened the door. When I opened the door I saw a big banner across our door that said "Congratulations" written across it. I turned to my dad and asked him, "Does she just know that we just lost by 20 in the state championship game?" Standing under it was my mom crying tears of joy and she had a bag which she tossed to me and told me to open up. I opened it up and saw that there was an Arizona sweatshirt in there. I didn't get what she was trying to say so she handed me another bag which had my acceptance letter in a frame.

My first reaction was shock. "No" I said. "Are you serious?" My mom just kept nodding her head and crying. I had to sit down. I felt dizzy and was still in shock of what happened. The same night that I got my acceptance letter was the same night that Arizona was playing Oklahoma State in the Sweet sixteen and Salim Stoudemire hit his game winning shot to send the team into the elite eight. I called Jack Murphy right after the game and told him the good news. I heard all the cheering and screaming in the background and at first I thought that the cheering was for me but then I realized that it was for the fact that Arizona was on their way to the Elite eight.

After I talked to Murph, he handed the phone to Associate head Coach Jim Rosborough. I told him I had received my acceptance letter and that I would be attending U of A. "Congratulations", he said. "You're a wildcat now". I was beyond happy. I was practically giddy. I was still in shock and I would be for a little while. When I woke up the next day I knew that this was real, not a fantasy and it was actually happening and this was even more unbelievable.

School kept going by faster and faster and now that I had been officially accepted to the University of Arizona, I started to carry myself differently around school. I had a lot more confidence in myself when I did things and I acted differently and I knew that this was too good of an opportunity to pass up. I started practicing more and more and shooting as often as I could because I knew that even though I am a walk-on, I had to be ready both physically and mentally when I went down to U of A.

As school came down to an end I finally told my friends and other people what my college plans were and what had happened to me.

Not surprisingly I got the same response from the majority of the people that I told. "You're not big enough, you're not strong enough, and you're going to get taken to school". Other people kept saying "We'll see you at a junior college a year from now", thinking that I wouldn't be able to hack it with the best of the best.

There were some people that were genuinely happy for me and the fact that I had been given the opportunity to go to college, but the majority of the people that I told didn't really seem to care and I had to accept the fact that that's reality and people were either going to hate it or love it. Either way, I knew what lied ahead for me and I knew what I had to do to get ready to go down there and make it the start of an unbelievable experience.

Graduation finally came and I knew now that everyday after I graduated was precious time and couldn't be wasted because the summer was coming up fast and school was going to start even faster. I couldn't believe I was finally done with high school and ready to move on and embark on what was ahead for me.

To start off the summer before my freshman year, I got invited to Coach Olson's Elite basketball camp which featured the top high school competition, former U of A players coming back to be counselors, and some of the top NBA players who had previously played. The NBA players that attended the elite skills camp were Richard Jefferson, Luke Walton, Andre Iguoadala, Jason Terry, and Mike Bibby. As the camp first started off, I was with about 75 other high school basketball players all gathered up in Mckale Court and we were all ready to start doing drills in the camp. Before the camp started off, Coach Olson had former player Steve Kerr say a few words about the time he had in college and what type of experience he gained from playing under Coach Olson.

The one thing that I noticed was that out of everything he said he noted that playing for Coach Olson made him into who he is today and turned him into a man. It made me realize to pay attention carefully to him and all the other great players that had come out of there and really listen to what they had to say because they did something right to make it in the pros and obviously they bought into what Coach Olson had been teaching and my goal was to buy into what he was teaching from the time I was there.

The great thing about the elite camp was that besides doing the drills like ball handling, defensive sliding, and continuous shooting drills, I could really get a feel of what practices were going to be like, how the coaches interacted with players, and things that I would be doing to contribute in practice. The other great thing about the camp was being able to play in the pickup games with some of the pros that had left and learn things from them as well. However, out of all the pros that were there and all the great players that had left, the person that I learned a great deal from in the three days that I was there was from a former walk-on, Jason Stuart.

I introduced myself to him and he was very nice from the start. He gave me great advice from the moment I met him until the day that I left to go back home. The one thing that I remember him telling me was to enjoy every moment that you have and at the same time work hard because no matter how much talent someone has; hard work will always pay off in the end. I learned from guys like him, Matt Brase, John Ash, Fil Torres, Jason Rainne, and Bret Breilmaier who was also my teammate for 3 years, because they were all walk-ons and they had been through similar situations that I had been through. I was able to meet our associate head coach Jim Rosborough at the time and he was everything you could ask for and more in an assistant coach, just an overall great guy who really cared about everyone he came in contact with.

I also got to meet my fellow freshman teammates as well. The things I had heard about these guys, the clips I had seen, and all the articles I had read about them in magazines and online was unbelievable. I saw all three of them together and the word I would use to describe them was talented. I could tell from the way that they played and from what I had seen on the high school level that all three of them had NBA potential and the ability to take their talent to the next level. When I saw them, I first felt a little intimidated because most of the people in Tucson already knew who these guys were and they knew that these guys were the next big thing.

I met all of them at different times throughout the camp, but the encounter that sticks out the most was when I met the last of the three guys, Marcus Williams. It was somewhat interesting how we met, because as the pickup games were going on the team that he was on got sent to the court that I was playing on. When that happened some of the other pros were watching along with some of the assistant coaches as well. The one thing I remembered Murph saying was for me to guard Marcus. I didn't introduce myself when the pickup game started because I wanted to show everyone that I could play too and this was a great opportunity because I knew that I might be guarding him in different situations in practice when the season started. The game was to seven, straight up by ones only. My team started out with the ball and I launched the first shot I got and I hit it, I came down and hit two more making it three in a row and they were all over him. I knew that not every shot was going to fall because that's just reality and when he came down and went between his legs then hit a jump shot; I knew that he was ready to go and he had started heating up.

After he had hit his first shot, both our teams exchanged buckets back and forth and we wound up being tied at the very end and it became a one possession game. I got the ball, took a wide open shot and missed it, missed it badly. He got the rebound, pushed it up the court and slowed it down for a little while. What I didn't know about Marcus was that he played point guard as well for his high school team, which meant that he had the ball-handling skills of a point guard and was in a 6'8 forwards body. For about fifteen seconds he just dribbled back and forth, between his legs and back and forth again, and then cleared everyone out. I had somewhat of an idea of what was coming next, he wanted to take me one on one and use his height as an advantage. He crossed over the defense, split the other defenders and then went up. As he went up, I thought to myself that I could challenge him and try to make a good defensive play.

That's when it happened; we bumped chests and he got the better of me, dunking right over me, causing other players in the camp to "ooh and ahh". After the dunk happened, the pickup game was over and as we all walked off the court; Murph called me over and introduced me to Marcus. He had told him I was going to be joining the team as a walk-on this year. I extended my hand only for it to be left hanging in the air for a few extra seconds. Marcus was looking me up and down several times before he actually shook my hand.

As he shook my hand I said "Nice to meet you", he stayed quiet and then asked me "How did you get here?" referring to me being a basketball player for the University of Arizona. "Kind of a long story", I told him. I tried to be as cordial as I could because I knew I'd be going up against these guys every day in practice and in workouts. I picked up on his vibe as soon as I met him. I felt fortunate to call him a teammate and knew that I could keep up with him. I felt like after that pickup game he had a little bit of respect for me.

I had my opportunities to meet Fendi and JP as well. I felt like JP was always insecure about something and never had a mind of his own. When I met him at the camp he was so quiet and awkward, almost to the point where I wanted to walk away and go talk to someone else, but that wasn't my style. I told him I was looking forward to the season and being his teammate. Fendi was by far the nicest of the three of them. He shook my hand first and from the moment we started talking at Coach Olson's camp we developed a rapport as teammates but also as friends.

He was this big guy with a unique personality and he was used to being the biggest guy whenever he took the court. Marcus, JP, and Fendi were all different but they all had a little bit of an ego to some degree and it showed. These guys had been put on a pedestal their whole life and they had people telling them how great they were in high school and how college was a pit-stop to the NBA. Obviously I never had that, I was the complete opposite, but that's why I was looking forward to competing with these guys. That's the beauty of college basketball, you get to see what everyone is made out of when training camp and practice starts.

Before I returned home for the rest of the summer, I had a chance to meet some important people at the Mckale Center. I met our equipment staff, training staff, strength and conditioning coaches, and academic advisors. Of course some of them didn't give me the time of the day because I was introduced as a walk-on. I really could've cared less who gave me the time of day and who didn't, all that mattered to me was the fact that I was getting ready to start this unique journey and all I wanted to know was ways to complete the journey Unscathed.

When I returned home and worked out at my local gym there was word that I was going to play basketball for Arizona. It was like one of those juicy rumors that you think isn't true until you see the person and then come to find out that it is true. A lot of the older guys who I had known since I was a young kid were beyond shocked that I was going to walk-on for the basketball team. "Are you serious?" one guy said. "You think you'll be able to compete at that high of a level?" another person said. I tried to avoid conversation about it because it was no ones business where I decided to play college basketball at.

Chapter 3

HOWEVER, IT WAS INTERESTING playing pickup games with some of those older corporate America guys after they had found out the situation. They tried to go at me harder than ever before, trying to prove a point that I wasn't good enough to be a basketball player for Arizona. I took it to them twice as hard; after going up against future professionals at elite camp it was a walk in the park going up against older men from Orange County. I felt like in the back of everyone's minds they thought I was going to hit the panic button and come home because I received minimal playing time in high school. I was viewed as "lucky" in most people's eyes.

When I arrived in Tucson again in August of 2005, I had an athletic orientation with the rest of the incoming freshman athletes. All these different personalities stuck in one big conference room hearing about compliance, the "does and don'ts" of college, and how to handle yourself as a student-athlete on campus. What it really boiled down to was common sense. "Some of you will not be here next year or the years after" the academic advisors told us. We were told that in college nobody holds your hand and you're held accountable for everything you do on a daily basis and every decision you make can affect you for the rest of your life. I was intrigued by this.

I looked around the room only to see smiles turn upside down and fear began to rush through people's veins. At the athlete orientation my three freshman teammates, Marcus, JP, and Fendi naturally walked in late to the meeting thinking nobody would care. I was sitting at the row up at the very top and the three seats were open next to me and they lazily walked up and set next to me.

Out of the three of them, Fendi was the only one who said a word to me for about fifteen minutes. It was a good month and a half since we had all seen each other and all Marcus could talk about was his tattoo that he had gotten back home. The freshman baseball players all thought I was another pitcher and I kept telling them that I played basketball and they all laughed. I was built more like them and I was dressed like them during the meeting.

What I also had to do was move into my dorm room. I didn't know what dorm I was staying in until the last day of the athletic orientation. But I was able to find a dorm and a roommate who also had trouble getting into the dorm and it all worked out and before I knew it, school was literally right around the corner. My parents were there with me helping me move in and get situated with all my things. We were all feeling different emotions. I felt more nervousness then anything else because this was my first year here and I really had no idea what to expect of classes or anything. After I moved in, met my roommate, and got situated, my parents left to go back home and suddenly I realized something; I'm on my own now. I can do whatever I want, when I want. There would be no one telling me when to go to class, when to study, what time to eat, what time to go to sleep. It was all up to me to make the right decisions in order to be successful.

My initial dorm experience was interesting. There were girls from all over the place moving into their dorms as well. A few girls came up to me, introduced themselves, and asked me why I came to the University of Arizona. "Basketball" I simply said. They looked at me like I was crazy and started busting out with laughter. I laughed out of nervousness but still didn't understand why they were laughing at me, I thought they were laughing with me but I didn't realize that the group of girls didn't believe me when I said I was a basketball player.

After my parents left I had my first team meeting with the rest of my teammates. The meeting was in our locker room and I was so nervous I was sweating like crazy. One by one different guys would walk into the locker room and it went from being awkwardly quiet to a huge family-like atmosphere, well for the returning players anyway. With my own two eyes, I was seeing guys in person who I was so used to seeing on television only so it definitely was different to say the least. As my other teammates talked amongst themselves some of them would stare at me, wondering who this lanky guy was, why is he sweating so much and why he's here with the team.

Slowly but surely everyone introduced themselves one by one and the butterflies I had in my stomach began to fly out and I was ready to get to know my teammates. We would practice together, play in games together, go through workouts together, and be there for each other as teammates. What was so great about meeting all of them at one time was that every one of my teammates presented themselves in a different way and that was a good thing because that means that they all had their own styles and different ways of doing things. That's one of the beautiful things of college basketball, in this locker room where memories are shared left and right, you have a group of fifteen guys from all over the country and all over the world who try to get on the same page and share the same goal; winning a national championship.

After I introduced myself to everyone, Coach Rosborough entered the locker room and addressed us as a team. Before he even started the meeting he introduced me to the team and told them that I would be joining the team as a walk-on this year. As soon as he said that everyone just looked at me for a second or two. My natural instinct caused me to be somewhat shy at first but then I kind of nodded to everyone and then he gave his speech.

He had told us that we have a great opportunity this season to do something special. We've all seen teams winning national championships and we all get to see how good it feels. I was thinking to myself how sweet would it be to be part of a national championship team my freshman year. As coach Rosborough continued his speech, he brought in Lisa Napoleon who is our academic advisor and handles our grades, classes, scheduling, and what major we want to pick. She handed us our schedules and a complete outline of the expectations and what the coaches expected from us on the court, as well as off the court.

After he spoke, Hassan Adams, a senior stood up and addressed all of us as well. I was learning first hand how things were done around here. He said that we were all in this together, as one, as a family. We huddled up as a group, stuck fifteen arms in the middle and yelled the word "Family!" It was the first time I was beyond excited to start everything, workouts, practice, and conditioning. I didn't care what was going to lie ahead I was just excited to experience it with these guys.

Right away I could sense the difference between my high school and college teammates. Guys look forward to putting in hard work and look forward to doing the little things. In college everyone's just as athletic as the next guy and the talent level goes up tremendously and I was ready to compete.

My freshman year could really be summed up in two words: A Test. Everything I went through was a test, literally. Mentally, physically, psychologically, there were so many different angles of the first year of the journey. My teammates tested me in so many ways, part of me always believed they wanted to see when I would crack under the pressures of being a division one college basketball player and quit. Off the court I was tested socially with my friends and in the class room on a daily basis and expected to participate and to maintain superb grades because I was a walk-on. Freshman year was a trial and error in so many ways. The coaching staff didn't know too much about me, except for what Coach Olson had seen that day when he came out to my high school practice. So if I were to fail and not meet expectations they would've been able to cut me after the season. My teammates didn't know too much about me, except for the fact that I was at the University of Arizona to be a walk-on, so when it came time for everything I was really put through a big test my freshman year.

When classes started there was a sense of fear because it's a foreign environment to newcomers. Campus was overwhelming to say the least, it was an oasis in the middle of a desert known as Tucson and once you stepped foot inside Arizona's campus things would change. My freshman roommate, who was a baseball player, had the same class I did and we walked to it together. "Are you sure you're a basketball player?" he used to ask me. "Yes!" I would yell back.

Teachers in college were different than teachers in high school. Of course they wanted us to succeed but at the same time it wasn't their problem if some of us made poor choices and chose not to go to class. When I walked up to my teacher and handed her our team schedule for the upcoming season, the demeanor immediately changed. She immediately thought I was going to have that "jock mentality". That was the theme on teachers face when they saw that piece of paper. What I didn't realize was that Tucson lives for Arizona basketball and the season and student athletes have a bad reputation in terms of not going to class. Professors feed off of this because it gives them an excuse to show the power that they have at a basketball crazy school. I had to prove to all my professors that when it came to school and grades I was all business.

I remember the first real encounter I had with Coach Olson. I received a phone call before my first class from his assistant at the time, Monica Armenta and she had left me a message telling me that I had a meeting with Coach Olson that would last no longer than 5 minutes. My initial thought I had at first was fear. I was thinking a 5 minute meeting could only mean something bad. The meeting with Coach O wasn't until the later part of the afternoon, so I had the whole day to be nervous and think about all the possibilities that could've happened. Before every class I kept looking at my watch as the minutes and seconds kept going by faster and faster. As I walked over to the Mckale Center I figured it might be one of the last times I would go there. Realistically I was thinking he was going to cut me right then and there. I mean he's a hall of fame coach so what would he need a walk-on for? He has the most athletic players in the country every year so he wouldn't want me; he would want someone ten times more athletic than me right?

My arms and legs were like noodles when I got to his office; I was thinking that five minutes was going to be the last five minutes I would ever have at Arizona. I waited outside his office patiently. He was in there with Marcus Williams talking to him. As Marcus walked out I looked at him thinking that might be the last time I saw him because I was about to get cut. Coach Olson walked out, extended his hand towards me and invited me into his office. I smiled nervously and followed him in there not knowing what the outcome of the meeting would be.

I was in shock when I walked in; he had the national championship trophy in there along with the net from that game. He also had pac-10 tournament trophies, regular season championship trophies, and various other tournament trophies and plaques as well as pictures of him and President Clinton. You name it he had it. I sat down on his couch and it was right across from a chair that he sat in. I know he couldn't see it but I was so nervous which was why my back was sweating so much and my lower legs were shaking. I had no idea what was going to happen after that point. For about 5-10 Seconds we just kind of sat there and looked at each other. I didn't know what to say to him, I was just hoping not to make a fool out of myself in there. I wanted him to take me seriously which is why I was sitting straight up and trying as hard as I could to look at him in the face.

After that little span had passed he looked at me and started talking to me. He asked how I liked school and how I was adjusting to college life. I smiled and told him I liked it a lot I just had to get used to the heat and the routine of everything. It was kind of overwhelming at first having a conversation with Lute Olson but I didn't let that stop me from speaking my mind. Then he started asking me about the basketball side of things and if I was getting along with my teammates and things like that. I told him I was excited to start up everything and I couldn't stop thanking him for the opportunity and how it was a dream come true.

All of a sudden it was if the whole mood of the conversation had changed. It went from being a conversation about school and basketball to other topics like my high school experience and recruits. Our conversation was supposed to last around five minutes; it lasted for about forty minutes. Halfway through our conversation I started to relax and just enjoy the ride. I could feel the tension and nervous energy easing out of my body and in return was one of the best conversations I ever had. He was in no hurry to get me out of there and I was certainly in no hurry to leave and we were talking to each other the whole time. A part of me was still in shock because I was having a conversation with Lute Olson; I had to get everything out of my head and realize that this man was my coach now and the expectations he had for me along with my teammates were second to none. Words can't describe the emotions and feelings I had going into that meeting and then carrying on the conversation with a legend. I was glad our conversation got extended.

Obviously I was asking the majority of the questions because I was curious about certain things like what my role on the team would be. I knew I would have that label as being a walk-on but I wanted to hear specifically from him what my role would be and he told me right then and there that the majority of my work would be done in practice and for some reason that really intrigued me because I loved to practice.

The one thing I took from the meeting with Coach O was the message he told me right before we ended our conversation. I asked him for some advice about approaching the season and how to handle everything like practices, weight sessions, class, and things like that. Coach told me that if I embraced everything that was thrown my way, worked as hard as I could, kept a good attitude, and gave everything 110% then this could be the experience of a lifetime. That was his point of emphasis during our conversation and to this day I think about what he told me. I think he sensed that I needed a little of his guidance because I was never recruited by him or had an in house visit so this was really the first time I had to get the know the guy. I wish I could've met with him everyday just to get advice from him.

The guy has so much knowledge about life it's scary; growing up I heard that Lute Olson was always the "Gentleman's Coach" and I finally had my chance first hand to witness it and talk to the guy for a good amount of time. That meeting I had with Coach Olson really changed my attitude about a lot of different things and how I approached things in life. Everyday when I would do something I would think about those words that Coach O told me and try to apply it.

As we ended the meeting he told me to enjoy the rest of the week and keep working hard in class and if I had any questions to not be afraid to ask. That's one of the things I loved about Coach was the fact that he never treated me like a walk-on; he treated me like I was a starter or an All-American. That's why he's one of the best coaches ever and he really is the "Gentleman's Coach."

After that meeting I called my mom and told her what just happened. Being a mom, her natural reaction was ecstatic and excitement. She kept telling me to use that meeting as a starting point so I can become close with Coach Olson and bond with him. I told a few of my teammates about the meeting and they were surprised. I was pretty surprised. It's not everyday a man of Lute Olson's stature meets with a walk-on for more than 5 minutes. Marcus had some interesting feedback for me when I told him about the meeting. "He feels sorry for you" he used to say as he smiled that sly grin, referring to my status on the team as a walk-on.

Marcus was by far the rudest of all my teammates, giving off that arrogant vibe wherever he was at, he also gave me a nickname my freshman year. Whenever we were all together he would simply call me "walk-on". He had no problem saying it; I had a problem when he said it I just never spoke up. The reasoning for this was because he said I had to earn the right to be called by my last name. I never understand it at first but I began to after a little while, Marcus felt like he had more power than me because he was the big recruit on scholarship and would someday have a chance at playing professional basketball. He used to say it to my face everywhere we were. The time it hurt the most was when I was walking to a workout one day and I saw Marcus and JP out of the corner of my eye about 30 yards away.

He looked at me and waived, signaling me to come over. There was also a group of girls with him and as I walked over and said hey he looked at the girls and said "Remember that guy I was telling you about? This is him, his name is walk-on". Everyone began to laugh, I just walked away. I knew right then and there that this guy didn't care about anyone except himself. He was self-centered and if you couldn't help him or do something for him then he didn't want to have anything to do with you.

I got called to my first workout from Coach Pastner later that week. I was a little nervous but at the same time it was another great opportunity for me to get to gel with my teammates and do anything I could to help out the team. Coach Pastner was the post player coach so what he used me for in the majority of his workouts was to play defense on the big guys, feed them in the posts, or to be a guard and have them set screens for me and practice game-like situations. I learned so much from a half-hour workout with four guys.

At first I had trouble keeping up because I had to get used to the pace at which these guys were going at and I knew that I didn't have much time because the season was coming up shortly, so I had to learn quickly. After the workout my shirt was just drenched with sweat, and my body was a little sore because I wasn't used to anything like that before.

It was pretty basic in the beginning. Go to class, go to lifting, do as many workouts as I could wherever I was needed, then take care of whatever things I needed to do during the day. I was embedded with this routine of working out at an extreme level from day one and I tried to do as much as I can with the time I was given for anything. Jack Murphy, the guy who helped me to walk-on used to call me into his office every other few days during my first month of school.

Chapter 4

H E WOULD CALL ME into his office to check up on me, making sure I was finding everything on campus alright, my teammates were treating me good, and I was overall doing well. He used to class check all of us on his university issued golf cart and when he would see me he would do interesting things. Sometimes when I'd be talking to some girls or friends he would make me do pushups on the concrete. There were days when it was over a hundred degrees and the blacktop was very hot and I used to plea with him to not do the pushups. His response to me was "you said you'd do anything to be a part of this team". That was my cue to put my book bag down and start doing pushups.

It was definitely humiliating and embarrassing. Friends would ask me why I gave in to that type of stuff. I never thought I had a choice, in the back of my mind if I said no and didn't jump when he said jump I thought he would tell Coach Olson which would lead to me getting cut.

As the season approached, we had practice twice a week for about forty-five minutes to an hour because we were only allowed to practice for a minimum two hours a week. The first couple of practices during August and September were somewhat short, yet we accomplished so much in the time that we had. My first practice that I went through was a great experience because I didn't really know what I was going to be doing so I just took everything in and played as hard as I could.

We started off with stretching, ball-handling, and then doing a one on one full-court drill. This drill was unique because we have a team full of great players and to match up with someone was very difficult because all of them were so athletic and a lot bigger than me. But I knew that being in my position I couldn't back down from anyone, especially on the first day that I took the practice floor. I got matched up with Fendi, who was one of my freshman teammates who was also '6 7 and 240 pounds and built like an NBA player. The one thing that I had going for me was that he had never played against me before so he didn't really know how I was going to play him on defense.

The drill was fast and intense and I had to slide my feet as quick as I could and make him work while at the same time making myself work too. I knew that because I was a scrappy player I could do everything I could to knock it out of his hands as quick as I could, and every time I saw a loose ball on the floor my instincts told me to dive as quick as I could to not let the other person get it. I'll never forget the reaction of the coaches when I beat him to the loose ball and dove on it and he didn't dive. The maddest coach by far was Coach Pastner. At first I thought he was screaming at me because he was looking at both of us, but then he started to turn to Fendi. The coaches kept telling me to work hard and keep pushing through.

The first practice was interesting for me because I stuck out from my other teammates. I didn't have any practice clothes yet, no nametag on my locker, just a few Arizona basketball shirts and my old blue and white blank jersey from that elite basketball camp I attended during the summertime. I thought it was funny because it was almost like I had to earn everything at Arizona from my clothes to the right to be called by my last name. When I received my jersey after one of our workouts everything changed. I felt like I was "in". My confidence went up a whole level and in my world it was special. I was even so excited I wore my practice jersey and shorts to class one day. I literally felt like I was on cloud nine for a few days because I had received all this rare clothing that no one else could buy.

After the drill had ended we started to scrimmage and because this was my first practice, I was off to the side observing before my name got called to take the practice floor. I observed a whole lot during that practice, especially the way Coach Olson communicated with us. He made it known that he wanted things done a certain way and if you couldn't do them you were next to me on the sideline.

As practice ended Coach Olson Called us to half court and we brought it in as a group and said "family" again. That's what we were; a family, a group of individuals who were always there for each other as teammates but more importantly as friends. I often wondered if some of my teammates even knew what the word family meant.

The days that we didn't have practice or workouts, we usually played pickup games for about two hours. It was great because it made us gel with one another and it was good for me because it brought me up to the level that I needed to be at so when the official practices started in October, I would be ready. Competitive juices always filtered throughout the arena because arguments were heated, games were extended several times, and tempers often flared over various things.

When I got my chance to get into some of the games and run I struggled at first. The pickup games were a lot different than practice because practice is so structured in everything that we do and the pickup games was a lot more run and gun and fast break The pickup games also did something which was important for me, it made me establish my role when I got out there on the court and made me figure out what I could do to contribute when I got out there.

At first my teammates didn't trust me as much because they didn't really know what I could do, and it didn't help that when I got out there the first couple of times I turned the ball over. But as the games kept going on, my confidence kept rising and rising and when I scored I knew that I could keep up with them and contribute in some way, and they soon began to trust me. There was so much that stuck out to me in terms of preparation for a college basketball season, from the individual and skill workouts to team workouts in the weight room to team functions we used to do. So much went into everything being a success and it was nuts to think that I was just getting a "taste" of this right now.

Before we started our official practices we had this event known as "Midnight Madness" which is a gathering of fans and it gives them a preview of what our team is going to be like for the upcoming season. Little did I know it would jumpstart me to have a relationship with the fans and student section. There were events that were held throughout the evening like a meet and greet with the fans, a public scrimmage and a dunk contest. I was looking forward to watching the rest of the guys putting on a show, until I was told I was going to be in the contest.

I thought it was a joke at first, until Coach Murphy had told me that they needed an extra body for the purpose of the contest. At first I thought it was going to be a waste of time because I wasn't blessed with the athleticism that my teammates had. Surprisingly it was a blessing in disguise, I got to take the court in front of a crowd of about twelve thousand fans and all eyes were on me. Before I actually attempted my dunk, I decided to pump up the crowd for about a minute or so. I brought the arena to their feet only to miss my dunk, causing my teammates to laugh but as I purposely fell to the ground I started doing sit-ups in front of everyone. That was the first time I really felt embraced by my teammates. A few of them were recording it with their camcorders and some of the guys were taking pictures of me. I looked over and the coaches were laughing, it was one of those memories I could look back on and say I had the guts to do something out of the ordinary.

I transitioned from Midnight Madness to my first official college basketball practice. Everything I had heard about the official practices was true. At that time it was the most intense two and a half hour workout I'd ever experienced in my life. Intensity started to rise as soon as we got done stretching. All of the coach's demeanors changed from playful to business-like and now it became training camp. For the next 5 weeks I was going to experience something that most kids don't go through.

I'll never forget the look on my parents faces as they were sitting courtside watching me go through the grueling workout with the team. At dinner later that night they admitted to me that they were concerned for me and if I needed anything to call. I didn't get where they were coming from because I thought it was fine, of course it's a long season but I figured as soon as my body got used to the grind of these long practices then I'd be fine.

We had practice six days a week and what it came down to was really a test of wills between coaches and players. Coach Olson wanted to see who's going to contribute and who will be on the bench next to him and the rest of the staff. As the workouts progressed, the intensity went up and attitudes became more intense as well.

During position work I was battling for a rebound with Jesus Verdejo, another guard on our team. I accidentally tripped him and got the rebound over him and it made him frustrated. After the play he told me that my shoe was untied so I bent down to tie it; when I looked up his right fist had came across my face and almost broken my jaw. I remember falling back down as some of my teammates just stood and watched. I couldn't believe he did that; he was yelling at me and saying random things about how I intentionally tried to take him out and all this and all that. I just tried walking away and continuing the practice. Coach Ros came up to me after practice and told me he would talk to him; he did, and the next day Jesus apologized.

I wasn't as frustrated with Jesus hitting me in the face as I was with my teammates just standing there and watching as I was on the ground in pain. Besides our trainer Justin, nobody came to see if I was ok. It goes back to the team credo of "family". We said this at the end of every huddle in our practices or games, but when a player or "family member" is down and none of the "brothers" comes to help that becomes frustrating, and I know I was the new freshman walk-on but I would've thought someone would've been there to help me up.

Looking back on it I'm glad Jesus hit me, I needed that to shake myself up and if that's how they wanted to play then I was up for it. Jesus' apology was something short of sad, he didn't even look me in the face and say he was sorry for intentionally hitting me, instead he looked down the whole time and felt he "had to" apologize because he didn't want to get suspended or in trouble by the coaching staff. In the end the coaches always find out when something like this happens but I thought it was sad he didn't have the spine to make it sincere.

Before we played our first pre-season game, which was still a few weeks away we ate our meals together as a team. Usually meals were so quiet because we were all so tired from practice but guys were talking about the incident between Jesus and myself and obviously laughing at me for the way everything went down. Of course being a walk-on I had two choices; sit there and take it or try and justify that him hitting me was wrong to a bunch of that guys that really didn't care.

During one of our meals, Hassan, a senior was sitting next to me and told me that things like this happen sometimes due to attitudes and things of that nature, but I knew it went beyond that though. Jesus took that mentality of seeing someone who was physically weaker than him on the court and took advantage of it, because the reality was that most of my teammates were on scholarship and that's what they're supposed to do to the walk-ons.

There were so many instances in practice a walk-on will always have hope of receiving legitimate playing time when he thinks he's doing something good or making progress. But, when the system kicks in and natural selection takes over I wind up at square one again which is being called "walk-on" and getting struck in the face for tripping a guy on accident.

After those initial grueling practices my freshman year I used to ask myself two questions before I went to bed every night: "Did you get better today and am I this team's whipping boy?" I lost so much sleep asking myself that second question because I asked to be a part of this team so bad but I felt like I was on this journey that was leading me to embarrassment and me getting hit in the face every now and then. I figured this had to get better some way. Everything I did I tried taking that "light at the end of the tunnel" mentality because it's not easy being in a new place with guys who you don't even know, then as one of them doesn't give you respect and calls you a degrading nickname and another teammate hits you for no apparent reason it makes the journey that much harder, but that's the beauty of a journey, it's a marathon not a sprint.

Things started to look up as we had our first pre-season game. I felt like I was getting better during practices and I had started to make a name for myself. Ironically my teammates, besides Marcus, called me Bagga or "Baggs", not David. I would be introduced as Bagga to random people, I didn't really care I just got curious about it because going through life by your last name is interesting to say the least, I had been through so much so quick as a freshman nothing really phased me. The only person who called me David was Coach

Olson. At one of our team meals the mood was surprisingly good after a long three hour practice; guys were upbeat because we had food and the next day off.

Hassan started talking and making jokes about me and other things and naturally others jumped in, but it was playful and innocent roasting. He said he wanted to give me a nickname that would stick and that "Baggs" was ok but I needed something else to add to my walk-on swagger. For about an hour guys tried to say random things about what I should be called. "How about David?" I said. They all looked at me and shook their heads. Hassan looked around and decided to call me "Trash Baggs".

I couldn't do anything but laugh when he gave me that nickname. I asked him why he wanted to call me "Trash Baggs" and he just shrugged his shoulders and patted me on the back like a good teammate would. Of course that didn't stop other guys from talking. "You get the garbage playing time and garbage girls", one of my teammates said. I was at that point where I had to let it roll off my sleeve, I could go around the room and call out guys and personally attack them but it wasn't my style, especially with guys who are physically stronger than I am.

I left that team meal that night and I made progress with my teammates, I was known as "Trash Baggs" for a few days and just like anything else it settled down after the days passed. We were a few days away from our first pre-season game and I was still trying to figure out ways to build my confidence back up. I heard two words that changed my experience as a basketball player: Scout Team.

As games approached the coaches wanted the guys to be fully prepared for what they were going to face. Coaches took the liberty of forming a scout team which included me. We had to do what they did and make it game-like. I got excited because some of my teammates were trying to take advantage of me at practice or in social situations and I knew there was no better way to get them back than in scout team.

Being a shooter I knew the coaches were telling the starters not to let me score a point because at the end of the day if a scholarship player gets scored on by a walk-on it's extremely embarrassing, for them. I had finally found my happy medium, it took me a few practices to get used to the flow of running someone else's plays while still trying to run our own teams plays but it was something that helped me out on all levels.

Guys pushed me, physically and from a competitive standpoint; they talked as much trash as they could but Coach Rosborough told me if I was open to not hesitate and simply "let it fly". I understood what having the "green light" to shoot means. Sometimes I couldn't help but smile when I would make numerous amounts of three point shots in practice, causing Coach Olson to put the starters on the baseline and make them run sets of sprints, from end line to end line. It was gratifying to me because I found a way to raise the level of my game and contribute to the team on a daily basis.

That's when I realized that practice and scout time would not only become my game, but my big stage, my Broadway show. It was one of the few times when all eyes were on me during practice, it was a great feeling until the games started when I got to experience other great feelings as well.

I looked at our pre-season games as dress rehearsals before the actual show. That's really what pre-season games were; they were games to see if we were ready for the big stage that was known as "college basketball". I was anxious for the pre-season games because I wanted to see Coach Olson's methods put to use in something other than a practice situation, and I know all the guys wanted to go against someone else for a change.

Knowing I wasn't going to play that much wasn't a surprise to me. I had waited my whole life for this moment, even if it was the pre-season. Just being one of those guys on the bench meant so much to me. I had to develop a routine to stay ready just in case my number ever was called upon before the other team surrendered with the white flag. I usually got to the arena three hours before the game and worked out before the starters arrived. It was simple, show up before they do and workout first and then when they get here help them get ready.

At first, I was never sure whether or not I wanted to tape my ankles before games. Our trainer, Justin, always wrote my name on the board as the person with the first tape time but I never thought I needed it because I wasn't going to play. He used to tell me I'm just as much a part of the team as the main players are. Of course it didn't help my case for getting taped while my teammates were waiting and having them tell me to my face I "waste the school's money by getting taped".

If I wasted money for getting my ankles taped I could only wonder about the walk-ons on the football team and how they felt. I never understood why my teammates worried about a walk-on getting his ankles taped instead of the actual opponent. In the bigger scheme of things it doesn't hurt anyone in the long run by having a trainer treat a walk-on like the rest of the group.

Chapter 5

THAT FIRST LOCKER ROOM speech that Coach Olson gave us was incredible. I couldn't believe where I was at in my life right now, an eighteen year old kid sitting inside a locker room of arguably the best college basketball program on the west coast for the last twenty plus years and about to listen to a hall of fame coach speak. Coach Olson carried himself with a great deal of confidence and pride.

When I was hearing him talk I thought how fortunate I was because it's not every day you get to hear wise words from a hall of fame coach. I looked around the locker room and observed my teammate's body language every game. Interestingly enough, I could tell who was ready to play and who was unprepared. I wanted to be one those guys who were always ready to play, no matter what the situation was.

After his speeches we gathered as a team and said a prayer to keep us injury-free; I often said a silent prayer thanking God for the opportunity he gave me and put me in this situation. From the team prayers we transitioned to the area where we would run onto the court. Fans would line up near us all rumbling different phrases at one time. Little kids were standing with their faces painted wishing us good luck and telling us to bring a win home, elderly fans who had been season ticket holders for the last twenty-five years were trying to get a read on me with their eyes, and this was just the pre-season.

The crowd was incredible; everywhere I turned I just saw this sea of red with some blue and white salt and peppered into the seats. I saw students going crazy yelling our names and going beyond wild. Cheerleaders and dancers were putting on a show for the whole arena. I was usually off to the side rebounding for my teammates and shooting extra jump shots. I always thought that was one of the perks to being a walk-on, being able to observe the crowd and everything that came into the atmosphere of college basketball.

It didn't take me long to find my place on the bench, it was the last seat where the players could sit before our trainers and managers sat. I usually sat next to our trainer Justin. The two of us would have the most random conversations before the opening tip-off all the way to the end of the first half. He was one of those guys who I could open up to because he treated all of us the same, played no favorites, and just treated us all equal.

I could get a feel for a game before the first half even ended, I stated to pick up on things like if I thought we were going to win or lose and who was going to have a good or bad game. I felt like a player and an analyst in a sense but I wanted to show my teammates that I supported them while they were out there. Coach Rosborough would tell me in practices that when I was on the bench he wanted me to be enthusiastic and root the guys on.

I didn't know why he wanted me to but he just did, I never questioned him, he'd been coaching his whole life so he knew what made teams successful, if that meant me cheering like a little kid then so be it. I used to have this crazy thought that if I stood up and cheered for the guys every play and every time they did something good then the crowd would feed off it and would trickle down to the rest of the guys on the bench. Initially when I would stand up like an excited little kid there were different emotions. My teammates didn't know how to react to what I was doing, it's not every day you see someone who's enthusiastic about sitting on the bench. I understood that to the highest degree.

In some of my teammate's eyes, at least the guys who were on the bench, they wanted to be out there with the rest of the guys receiving playing time. I tried to tell the guys that you don't have to be on the court for forty minutes to make your impact felt on the team. The guys on the bench always have the most intriguing roles; I say this because when you're on the bench it's a guessing game. Besides me, nobody knew when their number was going to be called to come in and make an impact. I knew that if I showed some kind of support from the bench then it might have an impact on the guys out there playing.

The first time I got in the game was during one of our pre-season games. Coach Olson called a timeout and in the timeout he pointed to me and told me to check in. I was a little nervous at first because this was my first time playing in front of fifteen thousand people. After we got out of the huddle and got back on the floor, the one thing Coach Olson told me was to go out there, play hard, and have fun. There was so much to think about when I was out there even though the playing time was minimal.

As I got out there, the first time I touched the ball everyone was yelling "Shoot it!!" I knew that I couldn't just come in and throw up random shots and I wanted to prove to people that I can play too. The first pass I threw nearly got stolen and as I got the ball back the shot clock wound down and I had no choice but to shoot. When it left my fingertips I really thought it had a chance to go in but instead it bounced off the front of the rim and the other team got the rebound. The one thing that I realized was that as my time in that game progressed, I wasn't as nervous as I was when I checked in. being out there for the first time was like being in a foreign country, I was scared at first and I didn't know what to expect. I soon got over that and just played and relaxed out there. The time wound down faster and faster and the game was over.

We had won by a good amount and I had never been so excited in my life. The fans gave us a standing ovation and no one really left until we got off the court and the game was pretty much over. This was my first time going through this experience and it was unbelievable.

When I went back to my dorm room that night I was ecstatic we had won, even though it was pre-season game I had felt like it was the biggest victory for anything in my life. "Wait until things really get going", some of my teammates said. I didn't want to wait, I was so anxious, so excited, so fired up to get back out to practice the next day and get ready for the next game.

Initially that was what the season had become, one game down, thirty-something more to go. So much preparation, so many practices left, and so many more points to cover before we actually hit our stride from where we are now to where we wanted to be when March rolled around. Being a younger kid I'd always see teams on television like North Carolina, Michigan State, Kansas, Connecticut, and UCLA and you think to yourself how great it would be to play for them or against them. Then I would look at our schedule in my backpack and think "only a few games away".

A treat we had my freshman year was being invited to the Maui Invitational, it's often regarded as one of the biggest non-conference tournaments in the country. Initially I was left off the travel list because I was the last guy on the depth chart and rules for pre-season travel state that only fifteen players are allowed to suit up for games. I had booked my plane ticket home for Thanksgiving when I received a phone call from Coach Murphy telling me that I was going to Maui. I thought it was a joke at first but he wasn't laughing. He told me I had succeeded expectations thus far and that Coach Olson wanted me to go. Part of the reason I went was because one of my teammates was ineligible and Jesus, the guy that struck me in the jaw, had decided to transfer.

I called my parents and they were happy that I had an opportunity to get a real taste of life on the road as a college athlete. They didn't care that the ticket was already booked they just wanted me to go and soak in the moment. To be in paradise is one thing, but to be there and play basketball was something I was looking forward to.

When we were at the airport I was observing everything that was going on around me and thinking about how blessed I was to get to go to Maui for our first game. There were a lot of different people that came with us on the trip. One of the guys that came with us our athletic director Jim Livengood. I just remember listening to him talk at our orientation and things like that. Coach Ros was talking to me and told me to go introduce myself to him and get to know him. I was thinking to myself "why would he want to meet a walk-on?"

But Ros knew what he was talking about and I went to go introduce myself to him and when I extended my hand to him he gripped it firmly and told me he was excited that I was on the team and he looked forward to getting to know me. I was kind of in shock. I thought he was just going to shake it and move forward, but he was nice enough to take the time and talk to me for a couple minutes and started asking me how I was adjusting to college life. That made me more excited for this trip knowing I had a solid conversation with the athletic director. We still had a long flight before we got to Maui though but everything was about to kickoff.

When we arrived in Maui we had two practices left before we actually started playing. The games were being held at the local gym in Maui which seated roughly around two thousand people. Talk about humidity; it was beyond humid l in this gym, I think when we got off the bus and walked in we all started sweating. Since this tournament is one of the biggest tournaments of the year, all the games were being broadcasted on ESPN.

I had stood on the sideline for some practices but I didn't care about standing on the side for these practices because when I was on the side I was standing near Broadcasters Jay Bilas and Bill Raftery. During practice I wanted to go up and introduce myself but I was hesitant because I didn't want to get in trouble and dig myself in a hole. After we checked into our hotel we had a lot of down time, meaning that was my time to catch up on homework. When I was in the lobby studying I was taking everything in and this place was crawling with future professional players like Rudy Gay, Shannon Brown, Adam Morrison, DJ Strawberry, Ronnie Brewer, and guys that we'd all hear about for the next ten to fifteen years.

I thought when I joined the team back in August, all the workouts I went through were at a high level and very intense, I was wrong. I had the best seat in the house and I could feel the intensity from other teams and players around me. Everyone had to step their game up and rise to the occasion. The pre-season was done and now it was time for the big boys to take over.

We flopped in that tournament; going 1-2 in the three games we played. I was so nervous on the plane ride back because I experienced my first two college losses. I didn't know what anyone was thinking when we were traveling back on that long five hour flight to Tucson. All I knew was that this was the first time I'd be spending the Thanksgiving holiday with my new "family".

If there was ever a time to count my blessings and be thankful, Thanksgiving was it. We had thanksgiving dinner as a team which was different but nice. Being with people I had started to develop friendships with was almost like being with extended family. It gave us a moment to put away basketball and just relax and enjoy life for a few moments. We knew we had a long season ahead so there was no reason to panic after losing two games in a row; after all, it's just basketball.

I wanted to stand up and say how grateful I was for being given an opportunity to be on this team, I just didn't know how my teammates would react to it. Most of these guys weren't really the sentimental type, especially since we were all jet-lag from a long flight and we had just played a long, grueling tournament. So I sat there nudged in-between a few guys and Said thank you, silently; given everything that I had experienced so far there reasons I could think of not to be thankful, but at the end of the day I could wake up in the morning, look myself in the mirror and call myself a division one basketball player who's playing for a hall of fame coach and competing with future NBA players on a daily basis. That's something that's definitely worth being thankful for.

Every game was a unique experience for me. Being on the bench I knew I wasn't going in until the tail end of the game but it didn't stop me from wanting to experience something before or during the games. Sometimes as an athlete there are those games you play that you do something and somewhere in the future you can take a step back and say "I did that". For me, one of those games was when we played against the University of Virginia. The guys that were supposed to do their job took care of business and set the stage for me to get into a game, only this time, it actually counted.

Coach Olson had called my number and told me to go in for Marcus. There was still a good amount of time left to make something happen and get in there and score. Everyone told me in the huddle that if I got it just to shoot it and let it fly, I kept laughing but I knew that I'm not going to go in there and just shoot and not look like a team player.

When I checked in I felt a little bit of what I was feeling the last game which was a little nervous at first but once I got running up and down the court all that really went away. Then it finally came; JP called a play and everyone started moving at once. I came off a screen, he hit me for a pass, and everything else took care of itself.

When I released the ball from my fingertips I kept thinking to myself that this ball has a chance to go but it might miss. But that's all that I thought it was; a chance, until it actually happened. When the ball went through the basket I felt like everything I had worked for, at least to this point, had finally paid off.

I felt like I was on cloud nine. I had never felt this good and this excited in my entire life. Having 15,000 screaming fans cheer at the top of their lungs when I scored made me feel that much better. At the end of the game when we went into the locker room to get our post game talk from Coach Olson, he looked at me and he smiled and I looked at him and I smiled right back. For now this was the tip of the iceberg for me even though the season had just started, but I knew that there was still much work to be done. I went back to my dorm and people were clapping for me and offering to buy me dinner and things like that. When I went to my classes the next day my teacher came up to me and congratulated me on a nice shot. People were coming up telling me that it made the game. It was an unbelievable feeling.

My reward was being allowed to go home while the guys traveled to Houston. I got to go back to my gym and see all those corporate America guys who had initially doubted me when I first told them about my plan to walk-on. Guys were coming up left and right, congratulating me and telling me all sorts of things I had already heard back at school. It's funny, proving someone wrong is like walking across some hot coal unscathed; initially everyone doubts you because they're waiting for you to give in, then when you actually prove to them that you can do it, they ride your coat tails and you become that guy who everyone praises.

Watching the game with my family was an experience in itself. Already I saw the difference between sitting at the edge of my couch and sitting at the edge of the bench. My parents were acting like any parents would, yelling at the television and telling how much the team could use my shooting and of course it caused me to just sit there and laugh. As excited as I was to be home, part of me wished I would've been able to travel on the road with the team, I never questioned why I didn't travel but when I didn't travel I felt like I wasn't part of the team.

I would think to myself that I was doing something wrong when really it was nothing I was doing at all; it was just the Coaching staff's decision, nothing wrong with that. When I returned to Tucson they informed me that I was traveling for the rest of the year. I used to joke with my parents and tell them that was my Christmas gift. I'd take that over anything.

Being in Utah was a lot different then Tucson. Tucson was cold during the winter time, but Utah was freezing cold. It was around thirty-two degrees there and it was not going to get much warmer than that. During the shoot-around, practice, and pre-game meals, there was one thing on our mind; winning this game to get back to where we needed to be. Utah was known for producing solid players like Andre Miller, Keith Van Horn, and former national player of the year and number 1 overall pick in the NBA draft Andrew Bogut.

That was one of my favorite parts about traveling and seeing other arenas; I got to look up and see other great players' jerseys hanging from the rafters and hear about the times when the schools met in previous years. Sometimes I would ask Coach Olson questions just so I could start a conversation with the guy. I tried to soak up as many minutes as I could because the way he treated me was second to none.

If there was one thing I learned from traveling on the road it was hearing the variety of pre-game speeches that the coaches used to fire us up. There would be games where we'd receive messages from former players and then there would be those games when Coach Olson or an assistant coach would write something on the board in the locker room to fire us up.

Naturally it was easier for me to get fired up wherever I was at. All it took was for me to put on my jersey and I was ready to go into battle, but it's harder for people to get fired up on the road because you're in a hostile environment and you never know what you're going to expect from the crowd. My favorite part was hearing what fans would say about my teammates and me. Before the games started I could hear fans sitting courtside or a few rows up yelling some of the most interesting things that managed to make their way onto the court. In Utah, one fan told me I should've been the water boy. Another fan said "Hey walk-on! Walk-off! You suck!" I used to hear stuff like that and laugh. That's the beauty of being a walk-on on the road, people test your will every time and they want you to crumble in front of them and say something back which lets them know that they've gotten the better of you and they've won.

I never knew why this happened, but the first few times Coach Olson told me to check into a game I was always surprised. I knew when I started my journey as a walk-on that I wouldn't play unless it was the last two minutes of a game and the lead was big, but my heart would always race when he would walk down the bench and then keep walking to where I was sitting, look at me, tap me on the shoulder and tell me to go check in.

Chapter 6

THE MORE IT HAPPENED the more excited I got, especially on the road like against Utah when we were up by a lot and I checked in. I had never been in on a road game so it was a new experience for me. With time winding down I received a pass and my first instinct was to shoot it, but then I realized that I had to take my time if I wanted something to happen.

So I pulled it out, dribbled a couple times and tried to create my own shot. I didn't really go by my defender but I did pull up and get the shot off and as the shot clock wound down, my shot went in. I figured since it was December I got an early Christmas gift. I mean let's face it a seventeen foot fall-away jump shot is no easy shot to hit. When I hit the shot I turned to the bench and saw the guys excited. I looked at Coach Olson and even he had a smile on his face, I don't think he knew what was going to happen when the ball left my hand.

My freshman year in college was at the halfway point, Christmas break gave us time off from school but not from basketball, I had come to the realization that there would be no time off from basketball, except for a brief period during the summer. I was glad to see I had the highest GPA on the team. In my world that meant something to me, especially since it was embedded in my head from day one that I had to be the guy on the team with the highest grades. I used to look at it as a daunting task but if that's what the team needed me to do than so-be-it.

We rang in the New Year nicely with wins over Washington and Washington State. I got to see one of my high school teammates,

Chris Henry; it was always nice seeing old friends that you grew up because there was still that bond from high school. I honestly thought to myself that after we started out league play with two wins that we would ride those towards the rest of the season, I was wrong.

League play was a real life roller coaster, taking us up and down with unexpected turns coming at different times with an unexpected finish at the end. When we started league play in the PAC10, Coach Olson had us staying in hotels right across from our arena. There was a method to his madness, he knew that every game was bigger and stakes had been raised higher. At first I was roomed with one of our team managers, but that only lasted for a few games on the road. I often got roomed with my freshman teammate Marcus, or my senior teammate Chris Rodgers. Chris was an interesting guy to have as a hotel roommate, and as a teammate. He had this reputation of being an odd guy on the team and lived in his own world. But for some reason he always treated me well and tried to give me as much advice as he could, often calling me his "favorite walk-on" because I was happy to be here and embraced the role of being a walk-on.

He told me the perks of playing on a team that used to be ranked number one in the country and then the downside of when a team collapses and how basketball doesn't become fun when that happens. The conversations were interesting to say the least. When I would room with Marcus in hotels he would have me keep a lookout for him and he would have girls come up to the room. He used to make me promise him that I would keep quiet and not say anything. Naturally I did because I didn't want him to get in trouble or myself to get in trouble by association.

That's when I realized how little my margin for error was on this team. Although no one told me, it didn't take me a long time to figure everything out. When I would think about my margin for error I used to look at my hand and then my fingers. On a person's hand there's a life line which extends to a certain distance along with fingers. I used to look at the finger nail on my pinky finger and realize that was my margin for error compared to the guys that were on scholarship. It wasn't a bad thing it just put things in perspective for me.

If I went out to a party and started a fight with some regular students or had a girl in my hotel room on the road and gotten caught, then naturally I would've been kicked off the team because that's not what the coaches expected out of me. When my teammates got caught in some of those situations sometimes it was slap on the wrist which would follow with conditioning for the whole team. I still don't know how my teammates could invite girls into the room and then perform at a high level during a game the next day. If I had that type of athleticism then maybe I might have been able to get away with it too.

I started to notice a trend with this team; guys were starting to play for themselves instead of the team. Coach Olson and the staff were getting frustrated and practices weren't the same. Off the court issues were starting to hamper our group and slow us down. I never understood how hard it was for guys to get their act together and come ready to play. All of us were held accountable for one guy not going to class or one guy not turning in a grade check. Everything snowballed towards the end of the year and we hit this wall. All of us started to give into criticism that was being said publicly. Suddenly students on campus were questioning our team and shaking their heads out of disappointment.

"Welcome to the ups and downs of a college basketball season" some of the team managers used to say. I would go to class and sit in the middle of the lecture halls and I would get questions asked on a daily basis about the current situation of the team. It was almost like the students wanted someone to vent to about everything that had gone on during the season. "Imagine how I feel", I used to say to myself.

Sometimes in my classes I would put on my headphones and just pretend to have music going so I could hear what students really thought and what they had to say. Truth is, if my teammates and I were not basketball players I don't think people would've given us the time of day on campus. Even when times were tough during the season and we were losing students still looked at us like we were the rulers of the campus and I never knew why. You take the jerseys away from us and some of us are just abnormally tall individuals who make heads turn when we walk into a room.

I used to look at my own situation as a walk-on and ironically whenever I gave my input about other teams or players in the country people would just agree with me. It didn't matter where I was at or what I was doing, I could say really anything about a team and students would just nod their heads. That was part of the credibility I had being a member of the basketball team. Students thought that I knew more about other teams because of the fact I was on a team, when in all actuality I had no idea about other teams, I just knew that if we ever played teams like Duke and North Carolina I wanted to beat them.

As my freshman season progressed, this roller coaster was taking me on interesting turns. There was one point during the season when we had practices and I was the last one to leave the arena. I used to stay after and make a few hundred shots on this machine called the gun. Sometimes when we weren't running scout team, Coach Olson would have me shoot on the side or work on drills by myself while the guys scrimmaged. It was actually the best thing he could've done for me. I wanted my jump-shot to be picture perfect even though my form was unusually unorthodox. In fact, my teammates used to give me so much crap about my form until I started scoring on them in practice.

I used to stay after practice and make hundreds of shots on this machine called the gun. It was a God-send, it would throw the basketballs back to me and all I had to do was catch and shoot. Secretly I always thought the coaching staff would ever wonder if I was getting sick of standing on the side and then shooting while the main guys got to scrimmage, it never really bothered me.

The only time it bothered me was when I would sub in for a starter or a player in the rotation, do something good and then get pulled right back out to my headquarters – the sideline. That's when it donned on me that everything I was working for was an uphill challenge. I mean, why would I, a walk-on spend countless hours in a gym after a long, physical practice and shoot countless jump-shots on a machine with no one in the arena until my arms become stiff? What was the point? What was I trying to prove to everyone? It was a test, that's all it was ever was. I stated earlier that my freshman year

was a test and it was, my will was tested every day in practi᠎
other basketball activities, especially during the season.

I used to think when I was on the sideline shooting th᠎
snuck out during practice nobody would notice, and if they di᠎ ᠎y
might have moved on within ten minutes to another walk-on or
another guy that had aspirations of playing. But by me doing that the
consequences would've been severe and naturally I would've been
punished for leaving practice.

The thought of having a good and quick jump-shot is what lured
me back every night after practices and sometimes even games that
were played early during the day. Some of my favorite memories on
the team were when I would shoot jump shots late at night by myself,
usually around eleven PM or midnight. I loved being in the gym and
hearing nothing but the lights buzzing, my shoes squeaking, and the
sound of the ball I would hear going through the net. It would be
me, the cockroaches, and the rodents, basically a bunch of unwanted
guests in an arena occupied by banners, empty seats and hopes and
dreams. Stuff like this help me realize that during a season you have
to stay sane, even when times get rocky there's always a light at the
end of the tunnel.

Towards the end of the season we took this test as a team, it was
a survey to see what members on the team were the best at certain
things like best leader, athlete, attitude, and other things. We took
the test as a team and after the results came back they were posted in
the locker room. Naturally we all talked with each other about the
answers we put.

To my surprise, I got voted as the guy on the team with the best
attitude. When the guys talked about why they voted me for the
award, the feedback, for the most part was common. "It's not easy
to show up every day and go through the motions and then stand
there on the sideline for two hours", one of my teammates said. They
could say what they wanted but I knew that if any one of them were
put in my position they would've walked away. No one joins a team
and says "I'll be that guy who takes a beating during workouts, gets
made fun of on a daily basis by cocky guys, and then come to practice
and stands on the sideline for several hour hoping to get in". But at
the end of the day, that was my role, I had two choices, quit and be

"that guy" or embrace it and outwork the competition. The writing was on the wall.

After all that we'd been through as a team and I'd been through as a freshman walk-on, there was still something left to play for. We squeaked into the NCAA Tournament, being one of the last teams called on selection Sunday. We watched it together as a team and the mood was down. After the season we had and the off court issues we dealt with, I didn't think we were good enough to get in to the tournament. We were that team being talked about on every college basketball show, literally being made fun of by analysts saying we had "the talent but didn't know what it took to win".

Being in the tournament was an experience that I would never forget, partly because we were an underdog the whole time and partly because it was something that I wanted to experience since I was a little kid. The tournament to me was like an AAU event for colleges with the likes of ESPN, CBS, and other media outlets covering it.

After the season we had our last meetings of the year with Coach Olson. When I got the phone call this time I wasn't nervous I was excited to get in there and see him and I was hoping that my meeting would last another 40 minutes like it did last time. This time I scheduled my meeting last so I would have extra time to talk to him. When I walked in I sat on that couch again thinking back to that meeting I had in August. He asked me how I was doing and how classes were going and then we started talking about off-season and summer plans. Then I thanked him for everything and after I said "thank you", he extended his hand towards me and thanked me right back.

At first I was a little confused because I didn't know why he was thanking me; then he told me that he enjoyed my attitude and enthusiasm. That made my whole freshman year after he told me that. I tried as hard as I could to push the other players every day in practice and be a good teammate and it meant a lot to me that he noticed that and thanked me for it. I didn't want the meeting to end but it did; this time it lasted for about 10-15 minutes and I couldn't wait to come back and start next season.

When I ended the season things started to change. The routine was the same, continue to go to class, get up as many extra jump-shots as I could and just try to get better at every workout. People had decisions to make; it was crazy being in the middle of two guys trying to decide their future. Certain guys had to decide if they wanted to test the draft or come back for another year, of course nobody knew what to expect, if 2 guys who started the majority of the year come back then you have a good time, if they leave, other guys have to step up.

I was glad I never had to make a decision like that, my biggest decision I had to make every day was whether or not to do extra shooting. The only pressure I ever felt was in the classroom. If I really wanted to I could've taken the off season off, gone out every weekend and became a party animal. After a full grind of a college basketball season I had my work cut out for me when I returned home for the summer.

The beautiful part about being a walk-on was listening to my teammates talk about how they all had their own trainers who could "get them ready for the league" as long as they promised to take them along for the ride. Fortunately I never had that; I had my best friend Mitch. Ironically he was a student at USC and when I came home he pushed me just as hard as the coaching staff did in workouts. It used to be the two of us on the court, early in the morning, I'd shoot, he'd rebound, we'd lift, and then I'd condition. After it was all over I'd go home for a few hours and take a nap and come back and play pick-up games with some other college guys at my gym.

My best friend had different methods of pushing me to get better. We openly admitted to each other that when it came down to it, there was no point for me to do two-a-days because I wasn't going to get any playing time. But there was never any harm in being ready for anything that was thrown my way. Mitch used to ask me questions when I would shoot like "What do you think your teammates are doing right now? What do you think the competition is doing right now?" I used to look at him and say "I don't care about the competition I just care about myself".

It was the first time I had to take a selfish attitude when I worked out because even though the writing was on the wall in terms of my playing time I loved competing at anything we did. I could walk with pride throughout my gym and my hometown and tell the world what I was doing with my life. Ironically the guys that had bashed me we're telling me things like "They could've used your jump-shot out there" and "you deserve a chance". It gave me a lot of confidence being in the gym all summer just shooting constantly.

When I returned to Arizona in the fall I was a little bigger. I wasn't the nervous kid from Orange County who was afraid of his own shadow as a freshman. I was a sophomore, I had a year under my belt, I knew what expectations were, and I knew how the system worked. Being back meant that the season was just around the corner and we had fresh new faces who I could give advice to.

When Chase Budinger came on campus we became friends right away; we had so much in common. Both of us were from Southern California and pretty laidback, although he takes it to a whole new level. Chase and I knew each other before either of us played at Arizona, when we were in high school we played against each other and all he did was score fifty-one points in front of Coach Olson, who just happened to be in the stands during the game. It was one of the craziest games I had been a part of at any level. When he took his official visit I spent a lot of time with him and we became close friends.

I was looking forward to being teammates with him because he had as much as hype as anyone coming out of high school but he was so humble about everything and not once did he ever treat me like a walk-on. We'd grab food and sometimes he asked me questions about why I wanted to walk-on and I'd ask him questions about all the attention he gets from everyone.

The great thing about being back for another year was getting to deal with all the personalities I had met the year before. I thought it was interesting when I was put in classes with Marcus Williams. I had shared a hotel room and a locker room with this guy but I knew it was going to be an interesting ride to share a class room with a guy who thought he was too good for anything. Surprisingly we bonded at first; he stopped calling me "walk-on" and actually engaged me in conversations about how I was and tried to get to know me.

Then he would ask me to do assignments for him and write his papers. There was always a catch. He saw how seriously I took my academics and tried to explain to me why he needed me to do his papers for him by telling me it was my role and I should embrace being "that guy". Clearly nothing had changed except the fact that his head got bigger over the summer because he was getting NBA attention from the previous season. He used to tell me that he had to have a great year because he didn't want to face the downhill slide in college basketball that's known as the "sophomore slump".

Chapter 7

EVERY DAY IN CLASS I had to hear something about how he was ready for that next step and how he wished he could trade places with me for a day so he could have time to himself and hide behind the pressure. When I told him the pressures I had as a walk-on and being the team's GPA leader, he would just stare with this blank look. He didn't understand where I was coming from; in his mind all he knew was one thing and it was just basketball.

We started out the season with this pre-season trip to Canada which was five games. I was itching to get back out on that practice court and run scout team and continue the momentum I had built my freshman year. As hard as it was being a walk-on, a part of me missed being out there with my teammates because of the atmosphere that basketball provided. When things went wrong academically or socially I knew that practice court was an escape from it all. It was this outlet that honed in on my problems and for a certain amount of time I could be myself and just practice and compete.

That pre-season trip to Canada helped me out because I actually got legitimate playing time in some of the games. I even hit a few three point shots and made an impact and as an athlete there's no better feeling than coming off the bench and contributing. Things were looking up from that trip; when we returned I had been informed that I was going to be the team representative for various student-athlete clubs.

At first I thought it was ironic that I had been "nominated" to be the basketball team's representative. Part of me felt like I was nominated by default because I often believed that nobody wanted to be involved in activities that can help better the University and the athletic programs. The coaching staff told me that it would be a great experience and it would be a resume` builder when I graduated.

Surprisingly some of the other members of the groups I was involved in like the Student Athletic Advisory Committee were walk-ons. I thought it was ironic that a committee would be hearing from athletes that don't play or play minimal. Initially I thought doing things like meeting boosters would be a waste of time and had no meaning. When I first arrived at banquets I could tell boosters wanted to talk to one of the main players instead of a walk-on. I could understand where they were coming from, they support athletics to the highest degree but they wanted to pick the brains of guys who would be going to the NBA, not a guy who rides the bench for 40 minutes every game.

But when I took a step back and actually realized how much these individuals do for our school and the athletic program, I couldn't help but embrace the idea of speaking in public at banquets and getting to know them and having them get to know me. I found another way to escape the pressures of being a student-athlete; by going to these social events I learned how to network and gained skills that would carry me over after I graduated. After these events would end I would leave with a stack of business cars and each person said the same thing, "If you need anything let me know".

As a sophomore, there was a different feeling walking around on campus before the season started. Students would come up to me and want to get my thoughts about anything and everything to do with the season. I had people wishing me good luck a month before our first pre-season game. There was a buzz that was on campus because we had been ranked in the first college poll as a top 10 team. Anytime that happens a group can go up or down, and after experiencing what I went through as a freshman, I was hoping that our team would take the necessary steps to be an elite college basketball team in the country and not just one of those teams who had the talent but couldn't do anything with it on the court.

I felt like the team we had was loaded with potential that could've gone all the way to final four. Part of that buzz was because of the ten year anniversary of the national championship team and with the team we had and the way fans expectations are, they only had a championship on their mind.

My sophomore season was full of adversity; we opened up on the road in a hostile environment, lost, and initially questioned what type of team we'd be throughout the season. Surprisingly after we lost our first game, we reeled off twelve consecutive wins and suddenly practice became this playful environment. The starters and a few other guys in the rotation would have dunk contests and various shooting games, and guys like me would have extra conditioning and then scrimmage for an hour so we could get our workout in too. Coach Olson and the staff were excited because we were bonding as teammates and playing together as a team. I'd never seen Coach Olson smile that much during those practices. It's like that old saying goes, "winning solves everything." During our initial run, one of my teammates, JP Prince, had decided to transfer to another school which meant I got to travel for league play and the postseason. Before he left for good, he came up to me and wished me good luck with the remainder of my time here and told me to "take care of business".

As a team, we started to develop this swagger and carry it with us across campus and everywhere we went. Even my head got a little bigger because I got thrown into some of our games at the end and hit a couple of three's here and there, and I thought to myself that I had "arrived", and I used to walk into classes late with my headphones turned up full blast and it would obviously draw attention to me. That's what winning does to a team and to certain people. Everything becomes better, food tastes better, guys smile more, and all of a sudden you're excited to start your days off and we didn't care whether we had a long practice or a short practice, who the opponent was or where they were from, we thought we were going to win.

But as high as we were, I began to realize that everything could be taken away from us in one instance. After we had beaten the University of Washington, we were changing in the locker room and we were all being interviewed by the media. Of course I got stuck changing next to Marcus, who was rambling on and on about his performance and how he was stepping his level of play up.

A reporter asked both of us about UCLA and what his opinions were of them because during that time they were ranked number 1 in the nation and a lot of people around the pac-10 thought they were the standard for the pac-10. I tried to take the high road and say they were a great team and we have respect for them. Apparently Marcus didn't see it that way when he told the reporter that our team was the "Standard". Out of all the things to say, why say that to the media? Just tell the guy that we respect them as a team and we're looking forward to playing them, instead he went off in a rampage about how we are the team people should be looking up to.

Words are a powerful thing; the look on the reporters face said it all after he had talked to us. Our confidence had now turned to arrogance and I knew somewhere somebody was reading that and later on those comments would come back and take us for a ride.

I remember losing that game to Washington State and just sitting there in the locker room. We had a boat load of games left and we just sat there like we had lost everything and then developed a hangover and carried it with us for the rest of the season. Often times on the bench it became hard to watch and cheer for the guys because we were playing so sloppy. Our vulnerability had gone up tremendously and for the first time when I walked on campus, I felt embarrassed to be a basketball player. Mentally we became drained, none of us were looking forward going to practice and instead of getting better we were just going through the motions.

I'll never forget walking into class, waiting behind a few other students and handing my professor a paper that was due. When I arrived at the front of the line and gave the paper to my professor, he looked me up and down and instead of saying thanks like he did to the other students; he asked me if we were going to beat the next team we faced. The last thing I wanted to hear about was basketball, that's how bad it became when we hit that wall during the season again, I felt like basketball was starting to become the enemy instead of the ally I relied on to be by my side.

The coaching staff was scheduling team meetings every other couple of days and we tried to figure out why we weren't winning games and why we weren't playing together. I thought I was getting free therapy with my twelve teammates; certain guys had little to say while some guys had too much to say.

For me the ultimate low during my sophomore year came when we lost to North Carolina at home. Before the game I talked to the students outside our arena and they were fired up to watch us play. We lost that game and it was the worst home loss in Coach Olson's tenure. The next day I went to the mall to return something, I thought it was going to be a quick trip and as I walked up to the register to take back my item, I was cornered by three fans that were at the game. One by one they started questioning why we were losing games and why, all of a sudden we had become this team in disarray.

I could only stay quiet and just say "we'll get it together" which caused the three fans to shake their heads and walk away. I started to question everything and I realized that losing makes all aspects of life interesting. Several months before we had tanked, I, along with my teammates were put on this pedestal for winning and life was good. Now, we were all on the other end of the spectrum and it was starting to leave a bad taste in my mouth. We ended the season on an ok note, winning our last 3 games and building some kind of momentum heading into post-season play.

Before we played our NCAA tournament game we actually had a great week of practice. At the time while we were in New Orleans scouting and reviewing our final game plan for what we were going to do we decided to see a movie as a team. Not just any movie, we saw the movie *300*. It was a movie about a group of soldiers banding together to take on an army of enemies during ancient times. That's what we were in a sense, a group of players who needed to band together to take on the field of 64 teams.

I got Goosebumps up and down my body during the whole movie and I kept having this vision of us shocking the country and the world about how we were going to overcome the adversity of this season and make a deep run in the tournament. But reality was about to hit us sooner than we thought; the truth was that we had lost some of our swagger we had in the beginning of the year and we had lost some momentum that was carrying us during our twelve game winning streak.

The NCAA tournament always reminded me that everything our team did during the summer time, the off-season, and regular season was for moments like this. Within the blink of an eye your season can be done and all that hard work we tried to put in could be long forgotten in a loss. Sadly, that's what the tournament was for us; within one fell swoop we had seen thirty games flash in an instance and our season dwindle down as that clock hit triple zero's. There was an arena with one side of fans cheering and riding the wave of happiness into the next round, and then was another side of fans who knew that the season was over and the group they saw underachieved.

Before the media came into our locker room Coach Olson addressed us as a team. At first he was at a loss for words, but then he opened up and started thanking the seniors for everything they had done for us and the way they had represented the team. I was nudged in-between Mustafa and Chase and as the other coaches started to talk I looked at Mustafa, who had tears running down his face. It was hard for me to cry because I knew I had two years left and I was looking forward to seeing what lied ahead for our team and for myself. I told Mustafa he was the hardest worker I'd ever played basketball with; he was by a land slide, nobody could match his work ethic.

The feeling I had when we landed back in Tucson was almost like being stung by a bee. You try to avoid it but when it happens it hurts for a little while. I honestly thought with the group we had we would have a legitimate shot at going to the final four. I had to accept the fact that we had underachieved as a group, it wasn't just one player it was everybody. I couldn't watch the rest of the tournament; since we lost I knew there was no point. I didn't like seeing teams that beat us throughout the year get closer and closer to their goal while we were sitting at home thinking what could've been.

We had one last team meeting and as Coach Olson addressed us I was ready to expect the unexpected. He said he was looking forward to next season and we needed to be prepared for everything. As the meeting ended, we were informed we were going to have one week off before we started workouts. The look on everyone's face was priceless. He left and we were left alone as a group for about ten minutes before we all went our separate ways. Guys wanted to go home and do what they needed to do before we started back up again.

I used to week off to condition and get my body ready for what we were about to face. Part of me doing that was because I didn't get the playing time that some of the other guys received so I had to stay sharp and crisp, and I knew that there was no off-season in college basketball, even for a walk-on.

The off-season workouts were intense; three times a week at 6:30 in the morning we had workouts in different groups. The first couple of days we didn't even do shooting or ball handling, we just dove for loose balls and took charges. The balls were sitting in a rack with a lock on it, we had to earn the right to use them, and nothing was going to be handed to us anymore. Coaches were testing our wills and it was a game to see who would crack first and who could survive the grind that we were about to face. Just when I thought workouts couldn't get any more intense, they do, that's what coaches do, they find ways to up the ante and challenge you to come along for the ride.

It felt like we had a year-round season with minimal time off and a lot of days until the start of next season. Fendi and I looked at each other and realized that we were juniors in college and it was time for us to step up and be leaders in some way. For two years I had put up with older players putting me in my place for whatever reasons, now I convinced myself that it was my turn to take initiative and be a leader on this team.

I ended my sophomore season on a high, making the dean's list for my performance in the class room and I won a few awards for being part of the committees my coaches had signed me up for.

I remember one day my body just being so soar I could barely walk to class, I had to get a ride from someone. I had cuts all over the place which either meant I was doing the drills wrong or that I was working hard. But I could definitely say that it was making us tougher as players even though we were practically beating each other up to get the ball, but hey sometimes that's what it takes to win, by any means necessary.

We only had a limited amount of time and by the time spring rolled around we were pretty much on our own for a period of time to stay in shape except for lifting as a team and what not but overall I felt it was a very productive spring and with the nucleus of guys we had coming back I really believed that we had a good shot of making a good run again in the tournament.

Pickup games were intense, we tried to bond and gels from the get go during the spring time games and it did that to us in a sense because we could really get a feel for everyone and what everyone can bring to the table. My favorite part about all the pickup games was playing with all the recruits who took visits to our school. That's something that has always been intriguing to me because they always ask us questions about the school and what being an Arizona Wildcat is all about and to know that I could give them as much advice as I could was a great feeling for me. As for our incoming recruits they were not coming until June and when summertime came it was one of the most interesting experiences of my life.

In the spring of my sophomore season, Coach Olson brought in Kevin O'Neill; a defensive minded coach who had a reputation for being hard-nosed and old school. I didn't know who he was; I just heard things from people that knew of him, saying he was what we needed because we were becoming a soft group of guys. When I found out we were getting a new assistant coach I looked him up and tried to find out what I could about him. He was well traveled, coaching in college and in the NBA for the last two decades as an assistant and a head coach; he had made a name for himself on the defensive side of the ball.

When I was first introduced to Coach O'Neill, or KO as he told us to refer to him as, I was in the weight room when I got pulled aside to meet him. One of our team managers introduced me as the team's walk-on. KO took off his glasses, looked at me for a few seconds, extended his hand, and said "I'm looking forward to working with you this season". I could tell right away he was trying to get a read on me. I asked him a few questions about life in the NBA and he smiled and said it was completely different than college.

I tried to get a read on KO as well; I knew he was going to have a different approach with us than he did in the NBA because we're just a group of kids trying to get ready for the next level. Right off the bat I could tell he was the type of the coach who wore his emotions on his sleeves. He told me if I needed absolutely anything to not hesitate to call him and it didn't matter the time of day it was.

After meeting I thought I might have a chance to make a good impression on this guy; I wanted to show him what I could do for the remainder of the spring and I dedicated myself to being ready for summer workouts. As the spring time continued to progress and the semester ended I decided I was going to stay for our first summer session and take a class and then go home for the rest of the summer. Unfortunately 2 days into our summer voluntary workouts and summer pickup games I got a grade 1 concussion and missed the summer session. I got elbowed by Mohammed right in my forehead and I was out cold. I didn't remember a thing that had happened until a week or so into the actual concussion. It got so bad I had to fly home and leave Tucson so my parents could take care of me until I was cleared to go back and restart my summer school.

Chapter 8

KO CALLED MY PARENTS three times a week, checking in on me, making sure I was ok and I could still remember my name. I learned a lot about myself during those three and a half weeks I was at home and unable to do anything. I learned that things happen for a reason and how you deal with adversity is important when you're faced with it. I could've easily said "screw it" and just stayed at home and taken the whole summer off like the doctors wanted me to do initially but having an injury is an uncomfortable feeling and the more I was in my house and in my bed doing nothing all day the quicker I wanted to get back on the court and get back in the weight room.

In a way it was kind of like starting over because the injury knocked me out for a little bit but I knew that with positive reinforcement and patience I would be alright. When I got back to Tucson the freshman had arrived on campus and it was great to finally get to know all of them and just be allowed to play again. I already knew Alex from our days playing together in high school so for him and I, it was more like a reunion tour than anything else.

When I returned to Tucson to resume summer workouts with my teammates, I was forced to sit out because of the concussion. I spent the majority of my time on the treadmill or in the weight room doing extra conditioning and after the guys played pickup games I would stay after and shoot extra jump-shots.

Summer workouts were different this time around then they had previously been before. I felt like they were mandatory to a certain extent, but if I didn't go it wouldn't make a good first impression on

Coach O'Neil and his only real impression of me was me getting a concussion so I had to erase any doubt in his mind that I couldn't get through these workouts.

Much like the spring, we had to be at the arena early in the morning but this time none of the coaches could be in there to watch our workouts. Our team managers oversaw everything and since it was non –contact I was allowed to participate. I could see how workouts were developing and everything was starting to change. All of a sudden we were on this routine preparing for the upcoming season.

Being on campus for the summer was nice; usually after workouts and class I would sit outside in a quiet area and reflect on everything that I had been through as a student and as an athlete and think how fortunate I was to come back for another year of playing college basketball.

For me this was the hardest I had ever worked in an off-season by far. I didn't even play that much but the fact that I was with some of the starters and doing the same drills as them and keeping up with them really made me realize how hard some of these guys work to get at that high of a level and also to maintain that high level of play.

After I recovered from my concussion I went home and continued to do two-a-days, playing as much as I can and just getting back to the routines that I was on before I got hurt, and before I knew it I was back in school and when we all came back to campus, we were in for a rude awakening when school hit. The day before school started, we were called in as a team to the meeting room; everyone was there, all of us, the coaches, the managers, trainers and strength coaches. I was re-united with Alex Jacobson, my teammate and friend from high school. He put a good word in for me during his unofficial visit, and helped get me to Arizona when I was a senior. We were told that we did a great job during the summer workouts but we needed to carry the momentum as we moved forward. "We're going to take a different approach this season", Coach Pastner said, sitting there calmly as he looked at each of us for split seconds while Coach Olson and Coach O'Neill were sitting next to each other.

My heart was racing, I didn't know what to expect, anytime a coach says the words "different approach" it usually means drastic changes are coming, and then it came out of KO's mouth; "I'll see you guys on the court at 5am tomorrow morning". When he said that, a few of us looked around for a second, then back at Coach Olson, then back at each other. I think a few players already knew what was coming but I had no idea what was going to happen at 5am the next day.

As we left the meeting room he also informed us that we'd be needing our running shoes. 5am meant we actually had to be on the court before 5am because our starting time was 5am. Before we started our new journey I taped a quote to my locker and wrote it down in my room which said "if you're early you're on time, if you're on time you're late, and if you're late, you're screwed". KO had a thing about people that we're late to workouts, meetings, and practices. He made sure he knew that his rules were enforced on us before anything even started. I was in bed by eight o'clock and my alarm was set for 4am. When I woke up, my roommates, two of our team managers, Alan and Jim were already up before me and on their way to the arena. As I ventured from my house, to my car, to the locker room, I couldn't help but notice that it was 4:30 in the morning and I was the only one in there. One by one all the guys came in; the mood was funeral like, all of us walked out to the court together not knowing what we were about to face.

Everyone's hair was all the over the place, our eyes were groggy, and everyone's legs were shaking; and there he was, KO was standing on the baseline with his cell phone, looking at the time and making sure everyone was on time which meant early. Extra water was put out on the sideline; guys looked around and we could all feel the morning air sneak into the arena. The team managers we're sealing off the court, making sure nobody came to bother us. When the clock hit 5am, KO turned his phone off, put it in his pocket and called us over to him as a group and told us expectations he had for us.

He separated us on each side of the baseline, with the court being the median that divided the guards from the post players. I had to run with the post players because I was slow-footed and if I ran with the guards I would slow them down to some degree. It was fine with me, I didn't want to be the weak link in conditioning that I had been during my first two years.

After KO separated us, he pulled out his stop watch and before we knew it, the quiet arena was full of noise. "GO!!" He yelled out; our group started out first and all I could here were shoes stomping on the hard-wood back and forth, guys breathing hard and the look of fear we all had. When we finished the guards went, it was almost like an assembly line, continuous for as long as we could go. The demeanor on KO's face stayed the same while the look on our faces was absolute shock. This was the most intense conditioning workout I'd ever been through, and it was just day one. Coach O'Neill was so intense he made one of my teammates put his shirt back on after he threw up on it and threw it away in the trash can.

KO made it clear to us that he was going to be the hammer to our defense and get rid of that "soft" label that had been hanging over our heads. I thought I would be one of the guys that would throw up during the first day but fortunately I wasn't. Guys were in pain, getting worn out, throwing up on the sideline and cramping up. I had seen a lot of things since I started playing basketball but I had never ever in my life seen or experienced something like this.

I remember the first week of school after we had a 5 AM conditioning session on Friday, it was like we had a month vacation during the weekend because they went by so slow and then come Monday morning when the alarm went off it was time to head back to conditioning. Every day was this new experience when we went on the court; for the first few weeks we had workouts without a basketball, doing nothing but defensive slides, sprints, and footwork drills.

The icing on the cake was the stadiums we had to do at the football field and the mile run we had to do. We lined up side by side and it was pitch black outside; the football lights weren't on so we could barely see anything when we were running until we hit the top of the stairs. Every step I took I kept thinking I was going to fall hard and the closer I got to the top I thought the fall was going to be worse.

When I would look down I would just see the coaches down there and KO holding the stop watch as he timed us and continued to push us. I had to run the mile twice because I failed to make it the first time. I continued to ask myself during the conditioning sessions if this was going to help us win a championship. There's a smart way to condition and then there's the boot camp that we went through. Coaches condition players for two reasons; to build discipline and get them in shape, but this was something entirely different. A point was being proved to us that we were going to be accountable for everything. I heard someone say the atmosphere of Arizona basketball was almost like a "country club". That all changed when KO put us through these workouts.

Every weekend when we would hangout was a group we'd talk about transferring or quitting; I even talked about faking an injury just so I wouldn't have to finish the conditioning out. I didn't want to be that guy who took the easy way out because looking back I would've been the guy that "couldn't hack it", and I wanted to be one of the guys that passed the conditioning and moved forward to the season.

It was nice this year because we had a new walk-on as well. His name was Lucas Spencer and he was really close with Chase and Chase's trainer Trent Suzuki. It was nice because I felt like now I could have someone to relate to in terms of someone who wasn't on scholarship and we formed a friendship when he started. He was a great guy to get to know and we bonded by going to our school's recreational center to play every day for about two hours or so before the season started; after conditioning Lucas would ask me what it was like during my first two years. "Completely different", I would say after we got done running.

We used to joke with each other and we would always say how the two of us "never signed up for this" which was both of us referring to the conditioning that we had to do before the season. But through all of this we had to use positive reinforcement because that was the only way we were going to make it. When negativity sets in it can filter down to the whole team and I tried my best to stay positive. Sometimes I would always think about the point of doing this because I didn't play as much as the other guys did, but at the end of the day it built discipline. I knew that if I could do this every morning at 5 or 6 then I could have no problem getting to class on time or going to lifting on time or making my tape time. In the bigger scheme of things it always comes down to how disciplined you are if you're willing to do it or not because I always knew if I was unable to do what the coaches were asking of me they could always find someone else.

It's crazy how things change within the course of a year, just when you get used to one routing a person comes in and completely changes everyone, which in return forces us to change, and then ones that don't adapt to the routine slowly wind up in the coaches doghouse. My whole routine changed when our early morning boot camp started. We would usually end by 6:45 in the morning and then I'd go to the locker room, change, go home and sleep until almost noon before going to my first class. My body felt jetlag and we were still a few months away from our first game. In my classes I started to doze off and take naps, causing my friends and professors to ask if I was getting enough sleep at night.

It was hard at first because the first few days felt like hell; my body wasn't ready to handle what was being thrown my way but the more we conditioned the more my body adapted to it and the more vulnerable we became. Expectations were getting higher; we had a mixture of young guys with a good group of seniors ready to lead and ready for the season.

My two roommates Alan and Jim, who were also two of our managers used to ask me how we held up during the boot camp journey. I would just sit on my couch, drained, confused, and sore and respond to him by saying "I don't know". Alan would tell me how much of a grind the managers felt when they had to wake up in the morning and they had to be at the arena with us, and they weren't even the ones running and conditioning for a long period of time.

Even though this was Coach Olson's team, KO did the majority of coaching on the defensive side of the ball. I always thought part of that was because he wanted us to adapt to that intensity he brought with us.

I wasn't a big fan of his practices when we started off; I felt like I was under a microscope with him and he dissected my every move and the criticism wasn't as constructive as I was hoping for. When we would put new plays in or go over defensive schemes he would often sub me out if I made a mistake on the first try, and he wouldn't let me rotate back in until one of the main players was completely exhausted and ready to be subbed out. But, by that time practices were usually over and it was a sign telling me that if I wanted to get my workout in I would have to put in extra work. I was used to that; the low points were trying to shoot after practice and being kicked off by starters who needed the court to put their extra work in. I felt like there were a bunch of dead ends and by the time I tried to do extra drills a part of me had lost interest.

We had conditioned so much my body didn't really need to do anymore than it had already done, but I started to get that feeling that anyone gets when they're not included in practices; the feeling of not being part of the team. So, I decided to head back to the student recreational center and work-out there.

Before practices I often ran on the treadmill for around thirty minutes or so, just making sure my conditioning stayed at where it needed to be. Combining that with a long two and a half hour practice and my body was done. Believe it or not, standing on the sideline or shooting on the side can take a toll on your body.

As practices continued to progress, I got thrown into the fire here and there, but when a few of the starters sat out because they wanted to rest or to prevent injury, I got my chance to go through a whole two hour practice, one which didn't include scout team. These were some of the most interesting moments for me personally, when guys like Chase, Jordan, Jawann and Jerryd sat out to rest, I started to regain the confidence I had during some of the workouts because I was actually getting more of a chance to be out there and learn.

On Sunday Morning November 4th, 2007, we were woken up about 2 hours before our shoot around at Mckale Center. When I woke up I could already sense that something bad had either already happened or was going to happen. Either way my heart was racing like no other when I walked into the locker room.

In Front of us was Athletic director Jim Livengood and to his right was KO. We had been informed as a team that Coach Olson was taking a leave of Absence and his return would be indeterminable. I was in shock more than anything else as was probably everyone else. It was crazy to think that he would not be there for our first two scrimmages and could miss extended time after that. My heart and my mind didn't feel right; I couldn't even focus on playing the pre-season game we had that day. When I went home to shower and get my mind right for the game after shoot-around it was already on every channel. From ESPN to CNN to MSNBC, that was the impact that Lute Olson had on everyone.

It was crazy, more surreal than anything else. I couldn't picture our games without our Commander n' chief on the sidelines in those typical blazers that he always wore. The game rolled around and people in the stands were also in shock, I could tell by the looks on their faces and expressions. Most of these fans had been season ticket holders since Coach Olson's early tenure year in Tucson. For them it was a huge surprise if anything else.

After the game the media came in and asked us questions left and right. We knew just as much as they did and nothing more, nothing less. I remember going home to check my face-book and I had about 30 messages about my reaction to Coach Olson taking a leave of absence, some people didn't understand that I knew just as much as them if not less than they did. The next day was hell from the beginning, from class all the way to our afternoon practice. I entered my first class at 11 and when I walked in I could hear people talking about it from all angles of the classroom.

When I grabbed lunch after my classes I saw the media cars from a lot of different stations lined up and interviewing as many students as possible to get feedback on everything going on. Everyone had literally panicked in Tucson.

Part of me wanted to call Coach Olson and see if he was alright, but another part of me didn't want to bother the guy, I know he had people bombarding him left and right about why he was taking a leave of absence. I didn't want to be another one of those guys. Coach Olson's grandson and our director of operations Matt Brase encouraged me alone with the rest of the guys to give him a call to see how he was doing.

I didn't even know what I was going to say to the man; I'd known Coach Olson for two years and I had never been as nervous as I was when I called him a few hours after we had practice one day. Unlike my first conversation I had with him when I was a freshman, this was a quick call. After I hung up the phone I remember thinking about all the scenarios that were going on in the man's life. When someone like Coach Olson isn't there during your everyday life you're not just missing a coach, you're missing an Icon and a guy that treated all of us like our fathers did. That's what made the man a hall of fame coach, his ability to impact all of our lives and now that he was gone for a certain amount of time, we had to bond together even closer as a team.

Chapter 9

ONE OF THE MOST awkward moments for me came a few days after Coach Olson made his announcement about his leave of absence. I went to my teacher's office hours inquiring about a grade and an upcoming test; he invited me in, closed the door and told me to sit down. When I opened up my backpack and pulled out my grade check my professor told me he wanted to talk about the situation with Coach Olson and our team. After I told him I couldn't go into depth about it and just as much as everyone else, he refused to give me my grade at first until he said he "felt bad" and signed my grade check, and later telling me he had a meeting to go to.

It was awkward for a little bit; the practices felt weird with him not there coaching, talking, and teaching. KO had his own way of doing things after Coach Olson had started his leave of absence; practices were run differently, and everything in general was done in a different manner.

For me, just like everyone else on the team, there were high points and low points when KO took over. When we started the scout team back up before our first official game, he wanted me to become that guy who gets under the players' skin during practices and makes them work; having me pressure the ball as hard as I could. This didn't sit well with some of the players. I got in altercations with different guys on different days. It almost got to the point where I didn't want to be out there because I had to start being a pest. He also wouldn't let me ask as many questions as I used to with Coach Olson.

A part of me felt like I was being an annoyance to him sometimes but I think he looked at it like I was playing catch-up with the rest of the team. But nobody realized that running scout team takes just as much work, if not more than running plays for our team. I had to mimic every move that a guy from another school would do and it took a lot of planning and paying attention to detail. Sometimes I felt like if I wasn't Chase, Jordan, or Jerryd I couldn't ask him a question. I don't think he had a vendetta against any players but he just wanted things done a certain way; practice time was precious, especially to coaches and if it's during the season there's a whole new level of meaning to practice time.

Being a walk-on I picked up on the way coaches dealt with players; I always used to ask myself those "what if" types of questions wondering if I were a scholarship player would coaches deal with me differently than if I were a walk-on? I hate to say it but sometimes being a walk-on made me feel like the team's whipping boy, especially during situations like these ones; I never feared going to ask a coach questions as much as I did with KO; I found the most unusual place to talk to him and ask him all the questions about practices, games, opponents, and life in general: The weight room.

Before the practices, when I would do my extra conditioning on the treadmill or stationary bike, which was a routine that KO implemented during the season for the guys who didn't play at least fifteen minutes a game, he would be in there riding the bike himself. Usually he'd be on the phone talking to someone about something that happened and sometimes when he saw me come in he'd put his phone away, almost knowing that I was warming up my mouth to ask him something about basketball. To my surprise, he answered questions about anything and everything, and of course, he asked me questions about my concussion I suffered when he first arrived, and about the guys and how they were feeling about practices and upcoming opponents. I was trying hard to figure him out and I know he was still trying to get a read on me.

One of the other low points with KO came during our second pre-season game; we had jumped on this team and the game was really over before it even started. At about the two and a half minute mark, the student section and remaining fans that were scattered throughout the arena started chanting my name, signaling for me to go in. By this point everyone knew that when I entered the game, it was a symbol that the other team had raised the white flag and surrendered, giving people like me, a walk-on an opportunity to get in. I sat there patiently next to our trainer Justin, secretly wondering why I hadn't checked in yet.

I was so used to being thrown in immediately by Coach Olson and it caught me off guard still sitting there on the bench and listening to the crowd chant my name. One by one my teammates turned their heads to my direction, looked at me and raised their eyebrows. I proceeded to look back at them and shrug my shoulders. KO, meanwhile was standing in the coaches box; he looked at me with that intense look on his face he often had during our boot-camp conditioning sessions; I tried to avoid looking at him because I didn't know if he was mad at me or if I had done something, slowly he turned his back to me and watched the game. That was the longest two minutes of my life; I never saw so many fans eyes directed towards me, I was just waiting for the game to end so I could change and go home. In my classes the next day, groups of students were asking me why I wasn't thrown in there. I had to hide the embarrassment I had on my face and brush it off. "Always the next game", I would say, even though my opportunity to get into the game was rarer than somebody finding a needle in a hay stack. I knew it was going to be a long season after that had happened, not just for me, but for everyone.

To my surprise, the next time the crowd chanted my name during a game; KO walked down to the bench, grabbed me and told me to go check in. As soon as I checked into the game, his eyes were on me like a hawk, he was watching every move that I made within the two minutes I was in. It was a bad showing on my part; I let the guy I was guarding score seven points in forty-one seconds and I committed a foul at the end of the game. Right when I did that, I looked over at KO and he turned to the assistant coaches and yelled something out. I couldn't hear him because the arena was still loud and I was on the other side of the court.

After the game I headed for the locker room with an embarrassed look on my face. Even though we had won the game by a lot, it's still embarrassing to get out there and then have a bad showing during that time. Within the hour I was home and my two roommates, Alan and Jim, and I were already making jokes out of it. "Long season", I said as I proceeded laughing to my room. I had the film of the game that night and it didn't leave my site until I had another opportunity to go in.

I wasn't looking forward to doing anything the next day; class, weights, or practice, but it was one of those situations where I had to just face the music. I know students and fans who were sitting in the stands had their own opinion but I really didn't care, I just had to move on.

Of course when I arrived for my weight lifting session my teammates gave me a hard time about it. On top of that KO walked over to our group as we were stretching, said a few things to the guys that played well; then his eyes made his way down to me. I tried to avoid eye contact as much as I could with him because I really didn't want to hear what comment he was going to tell me. I finally understood what it was like to be put in their shoes for a few minutes. Every time one of my teammates had a bad game or didn't play up to their potential, guys like me were so critical of them because being a teammate I expect the best from them and vice versa.

Although I was a walk-on, when I got the opportunity to get on the court they expected me to give one hundred percent effort, nothing less. Sometimes I thought games seemed like the easiest part of being a basketball player; I would show up to the arena before games, put that extra work in that no one ever knew about and then root for my teammates for as long as I could; then I'd use the crowd to my advantage and have them help get me in the game and I'd take it from there. But I don't think anyone ever really knew what I was really feeling every time I went in. It's awfully hard to sit on a bench for two plus hours, have my legs stiffen up, and then go in at the tail end of the game and pray that I connect on my one shot that I would get. But once I was out there I didn't want to score just for myself, I wanted to score for the fans, the student section, and of course my teammates and coaches. That became the goal; I was a team first guy and was embedded in the role of scoring for everyone else.

As the season progressed, we were winning some more games after we had started out inconsistent. We put together a nice winning streak heading into the holidays and most of us were looking forward to going home. We had a team meeting in Chicago before we played Illinois and we were informed from our athletic director that Coach Olson would not be coming back at any point during the season. I honestly thought he would come back, I thought he would be out for a few games and then once we started league play he would make his way back.

Practices started to change when KO took over for good that season; he had an interesting way of motivating us. One minute he was all over us as a group or as individuals for something we had done wrong or needed to improve on. The next minute he'd be praising us to high heavens, calling us the best defensive team in the nation. It caught me off guard at first; I didn't know what he was going to say to us that day or who he was going to coach intensely.

One of my fondest memories came when we were running scout team before we started league play. The starters were having the worst possible day in practice; they made our scout team look like the best team in the country. I was having one of the few practices of my life, hitting shots, playing good defense, and not messing up drills. When I stole it from our point guard, Nic Wise, ran to the other end of the court and dunked it, KO asked to see the ball and later kicked it into the stands. I put my hands on my knees, berried my head down and started laughing. It was funny to me because I always heard about coaches doing things like that but I had never seen it up close.

Things were up and down for all of us after New Year's. Guys were getting hurt; losing trust with each other and we still had a good chunk of games left to play. To my surprise, I would have a chance to redeem myself from the nightmare I had when we played against Cal State Fullerton and I was embarrassed by giving up seven points in forty-one seconds.

The University of Oregon was one of our first home games to start off league play. I had been sitting out the last few practices, nursing a bum ankle which I hurt during our shoot-around at the University of Memphis. Because our starting guard, Jerryd Bayless was also hurt, I had no choice but to suit up "just in case" something happened to another guard during the game. I wanted to sit out because I was in pain but realistically I had no choice; I was a walk-on and when things like this happened, I had to grin and bear it and roll with the punches.

The most unusual moment happened during that game; all of our guards got in foul trouble and with about thirty seconds left in the first half, KO walked down to the end of the bench, tapped me on the shoulder and told me to go in. I thought he was joking and then he yelled at me telling me to check in. I was caught off guard because I was so used to going in with thirty seconds left at the end of the game, not at the end of the first half. Oregon's point guard and my friend, Kamyron Brown, looked at me and smiled as I checked in.

I didn't know what to do in thirty seconds, all I was thinking about was not being embarrassed like I was the previous time I had been in a game. Someone must have heard my request because when Kamyron penetrated into the lane, I stripped him clean and Nic scored a lay-up as the buzzer sounded. I could feel the irony after I stole the ball from Kamyron. I never thought I'd be called into another game as long as KO was coaching us but to my surprise, I was. I sprinted into the locker room and started laughing before anyone else came in; event he security guard who was outside of our locker room had a look of shock on his face after what had just happened.

As the rest of my teammates came in, most of them looked at me, all having the same look on their face: Shock. I hadn't gotten taped for that game because it was a big game and because of my role I never played during the big games. As KO walked into the locker room the first thing he said was for Justin, our trainer to tape my ankles and then he told me to stay loose on the bench. My initial thought was that finally hell had frozen over, and I was finally going to get my chance to prove to everyone that I belonged out there on the court and I was thinking about all the hard work I'd put in.

I stayed on the bench for the rest of that game and we lost, but there was a part of me that was glad we lost that game because I was told I might have an impact in some other way than the typical end of the game, surrender fashion. I carried that momentum I had over into practice the next day. We had a two-a-day during the season and the better I played the madder the coaches became.

KO even threatened the team during our scrimmage, announcing to all of us in practice that he'd go as far as starting me the rest of the season just to prove a point to the guys that we can't allow ourselves to play bad. I felt special after he said that; it's not every day a coach tells his group he'd rather play a walk-on than the regulars. One by one the other assistant coaches and team managers were telling me to continue to take it to the starters and make my claim even bigger. It was one of the times where I had people rallying behind me in practice secretly rooting for the underdog to take over the reins from the dominant.

After that first practice some of my teammates were upset at the comments he had made; naturally anyone would've been. Sometimes nobody wanted to call a walk-on a member of the team, let alone be told they might lose a spot to him, that's just downright embarrassing. When we were in the locker room, a few of the guys looked at me like I had committed a crime for shooting so well during that particular practice; of course if the shoe were on the other foot I might have done the same thing but I happened to be in that situation. A few of them asked me to stop shooting because I was connecting on nearly everything I shot. One of my teammates even told me I don't do anything in practice compared to what the guys in the rotation go through. I wish I could've traded places with the guys in the rotation, even if it were a few days. I had a taste of it during that game against Oregon when I was in there for the first half but if life were like that 24/7 it would've been a different ride.

I was informed I wasn't traveling for the rest of league play because the rules stated you're only allowed to travel with a certain amount of players. I used to think if I didn't have that label as a "walk-on" then potentially I could've made the traveling roster, but rules are rules and at this point nothing fazed me anymore. It actually gave me a lot of time to catch up on my school work and have somewhat of a social life. The only rub was that when the team was playing on television I felt left out, and when they lost games on the road I couldn't go out and tag along with my friends because I didn't want to hear it from people who were out in public.

Initially a few of my friends thought I had been kicked off the team or I was transferring or I had violated team rules; all I could do was laugh when I heard people talking like that.

One of the great things about not traveling was being able to get extra workouts in during the weekends when the team was gone. Some of the team managers were nice enough and offered to work me out a few times but usually I preferred shooting on that machine we had used which was called the gun, because I could have time to myself to go in a gym and just shoot. I had been through enough practices and workouts to push myself without anyone being there and I didn't need team managers to hold my hand because it was simple, take two hours out of your day, put in the work I committed to put in and then move on.

Another great part about being left behind during league play was when I got to see Coach Olson a few times in the weight room. On the weekends, our weight room was a ghost town and beside a few other athletes rehabbing with their respected strength coaches, there was nobody in there. Before I would shoot, I would head to the weight room first to stretch and lift and a few times Coach Olson happened to be there.

I was like a little kid when I saw him come into the weight room a few times; I hadn't seen in him a few months and just to see him there, smiling and knowing he was ok made me ok. We talked a few times in there but the conversations were short; he would often ask how I was doing and how the rest of the guys were holding up with the season. After we exchanged a few pleasant words he'd go and start his workout and I'd start mine.

As the end of my junior season approached, guys were drained; I was drained and I didn't even play, the scene at our team meals had often become quiet and it got to the point where guys weren't looking forward to eating as a team anymore. We had been on automatic pilot since the first day of school and it started to catch up with us towards the end.

When we were eating at one of our last team meals before the postseason started, I was sitting with a few of my teammates and we had a conversation about life. It was quiet until one of my teammates asked me a question. "Bagga, how much do you hate life after going through the season we've had?" I did a double take after the question was asked. If I hated life as a walk-on I would've quit after my freshman year. Everyone goes through adversity, teams, players, coaches, and support staff. I could never hate anything, no matter how bad the situation became a sub-par season didn't give me an excuse to hate life. If anything, the sport of basketball was in my doghouse because of the year we were having and the way everything was starting to unfold.

Chapter 10

I THOUGHT WE WEREN'T GOING to make the NCAA Tournament my junior year, we had a respectable schedule with a few wins sprinkled in here and there, but finished towards the bottom half of the PAC10. To my surprise, we were one of the last teams to hear our name called for the tournament, it was more relief than anything else.

We had our end of the year banquet and a lot of us received awards team-given awards. It was nice because as a team we voted as to who got what award. I was fortunate enough to receive the "most inspirational player" award. I was in shock that I was voted to get it because I had never even thought of myself to win an award that didn't have something to do with academics, and I voted for my teammate Bret Breilmaier, just because over the last three years that I had played with him he had always done everything 100 percent and for him to play through a separated shoulder the majority of the season really spoke volumes about him and how much he was willing to sacrifice for the team.

The tournament for us, like the whole season, ended quickly, in disarray. West Virginia was better prepared than we were, from all facets of the game. They looked like the belonged there and they were deserving of a tournament bid. Outside of a few guys playing decent the game was nothing to ride home about. As we walked to the locker room I felt like there was a countdown until my college basketball career was coming to a halt. I was sitting in the locker room next to the seniors that were departing like Kirk Walters, Daniel Dillon, and Jawann McClellan. I saw the look on their faces and I kept thinking to myself how a year from now I didn't want to be sitting in the locker room on another team that underachieved its way to the NCAA tournament with absolutely nothing to show for it.

Our off-season was different; Coach Olson had made it known that he was coming back and he was ready to be our head coach again. Two of my teammates, Chase Budinger and Jerryd Bayless had declared for the draft; while Jerryd stayed in the draft, Chase decided to come back. This was the first time in the three years I'd been there that we actually had a break from basketball.

Even though Coach Olson was coming back, I was thinking about taking a permanent break from basketball. Given the way the season had turned out and how I was feeling from a mental standpoint, I was ready to quit. Towards the end of the school year, I was contemplating what it would be like if I quit the team and had my last year as a normal student instead of a college basketball player.

A few times I was so close to marching into Coach Olson's office, thanking him for taking a chance on me, and then telling him I was ready to go my separate way and enjoy my senior year. But as I took a step back, I realized that I had endured so much, from my freshman year until the current stage I was in; and if I quit on this team, especially Coach Olson, the man who gave me my chance as a walk-on, I would've gone through life as a quitter. I felt I owed it to him, and to my teammates to stick it out for one more year, and since it was my last year it was going to go by the fastest.

Changes were upon the team; we had a whole new staff as the summer came rolling around. Coach Pastner later took an assistant position with the University of Memphis; one of the teams that we had played earlier in the season. Out of everyone I knew affiliated with Arizona Athletics I never thought he would ever leave Tucson for another place. He was the one person who I thought would always be in Tucson as an assistant or at least be there for another five to seven years. It was sad to see him leave but I wished him all the best and thanked him for everything that he had done for me the past 3 years. I was sad to see miles go; he was a great assistant coach and great friend as well, I had known the guy since I was a young teenager. I honestly thought with his knowledge of the game he would've been a candidate for the U of A head coaching job in a few years. He had a way of interacting with players which made him a great coach. It was a shame to see him and Josh not come back.

In were longtime assistant coach Russ Pennell, who was well-known for developing players from the spots he had been at. Reggie Geary had also returned, he was our director of basketball operations my freshman year and I was happy to see him as a coach. Our last new assistant coach was a gentleman named Mike Dunlap; one of the most interesting men I'd ever met. He had been around coaching for a while and he'd seen and been through everything. Like Coach O'Neill, Dunlap was coming over from the NBA, where he was with the Denver Nuggets. I met all three of them before I made my way home for the summer and all three assistant coaches were devoted to us as players and as people. I originally went home early because I was getting ready for a summer internship I had applied for during the season which I had cleared with Coach Olson and the staff. When I came home I didn't get the internship; that was fine with me, it gave me more time to workout and go back to the summer routine I had been used to for the past few years.

Going into my senior year, there were two questions I had written down from two different people. Several times my father asked me on our drive back to Arizona "What have you learned from this whole walk-on experience?" I couldn't the answer the question because the experience wasn't over. He would ask me the question when we would talk over the phone, or through email, or any chance he had, making sure it was embedded in my head.

The other question I wrote down was from myself; I used to ask myself "How do you want to be remembered when you leave the University of Arizona?" Everyday I would ask myself this question, sometimes more than once, whether it was in the morning when I woke up, or right before I went to bed. I often lost sleep over it because I would harp on the issue so much and it was so important to me that I leave as somebody people would remember, not just another body that was berried on the bench.

I was blessed when I started my senior year with receiving a scholarship for the whole year. When I got the call I was beyond excited; I felt like my world around me was beginning to come together and there was no better way to start off the year than hearing the words "scholarship athlete" out of the coach's mouths. Everyone was talking about the scholarship. I was getting questions like how does it feel? Are you surprised? What does this mean to you? Being a walk-on, besides scoring in games, being given a scholarship was the ultimate high; I felt like that asterisk was removed from my name and people would no longer look at me as a walk-on.

For the first time in my life, when I started school, I felt like I was the big man on campus. A part of me felt like this was my time, maybe not to shine in basketball but it was just my time. I had put in so much hard work for the last three years and there was no reason to stop, especially after being given a scholarship. All the people who told me I didn't belong, or I wasn't going to be able to hack it, and said negative things to me came into my mind.

As positive a person as I was I never thought I'd earn a scholarship, it was just always something that I thought would never happen to me when I was at Arizona. My parents told me I was giving hope to all those kids who wanted a chance; I used to laugh when I heard that because the journey was far from over and the scholarship could've been easily taken away.

Being a senior, I looked at everything different, I knew it would be the last time I would have the first day of school, the first mid-terms, the first workouts, and things of that nature. As scary as it was, graduation was creeping up one day at a time, and we had a season to play.

From the first day of school, the new assistant coaches challenged our team, probing us and did everything they could to figure us out. They wanted us to take leadership to mentor some of the young guys. Guys like Fendi and I weren't used to being put in those kinds of situations; it's awfully hard for a guy that doesn't play to give out instructions to a guy who's an all-American and future professional basketball player. Still, I tried to take it upon myself from the first day to be some kind of leader for this team.

Coach Dunlap always pointed out to us, especially to me, that there are different types of leaders on a team. I looked at myself as a person who tended to lead by voice; I wasn't blessed with the athleticism that some of my teammates had but I was given the ability to be an encouraging teammate and I knew I could utilize that trait in some way to help this team out.

As a senior I looked around on campus and realized how rapidly the year was moving and I knew that I had to embrace everything around me for the last time. The best part for me was having Coach Olson return to the team and resume his position as the head coach. I would talk to my parents once a week and tell them how excited I was for the season to start because he was back.

It's one thing to play for a great coach, but to play for a hall of fame coach, who gives you a chance in life and let's your dream become a reality, and treats you like you're an all-American when you're the last guy on that bench, really makes the experience that much more special.

The first day of practice came so quick and my stomach had butterflies because this was my last first practice in college and I knew this season was coming quicker than people said. The first few days flew by and everything was looking great, we had a lot to get done and very little time to get it done in. At our media day literally every question was about Coach Olson returning and what it means to our program. Everyone was thrilled but we knew all good things eventually come to an end.

October 23rd 2008 is a day that will always be instilled in the back of my mind for the rest of my life. I remember waking up, going to class, eating breakfast, lifting, shooting, and doing my usual routine that I normally do on a Thursday. It was homecoming week, so the majority of the attention was focused towards our football team. But something felt different, something didn't' make sense and soon we would find out some devastating news.

I was in my communication class checking my email and I went onto espn.com to check the score of the World Series when I saw the headline about Coach Olson saying "Breaking News, Arizona's Olson to retire." I almost fainted I had to leave class and get some water. I couldn't believe what I was reading. Immediately I was getting calls from everyone back home and here at school as well as text messages asking me if it was true.

I remember going to the bathroom and crying for a few minutes and I didn't go back to class. My first thought was that it was a joke and everything would be cleared up by the end of the week. Maybe they meant he's retiring after this season or something like that. But no, it was true, and it was now.

So here we were, a group of guys about three weeks away from our first game and our head coach retiring. It became official later in the afternoon. We had a team meeting and the athletic director was there making sure we were all mentally and emotionally alright. I don't know how I made it through that day without breaking down. I don't know how any of us made it through the day without crying or something. We had a season to prepare for and now it was going to be an uphill climb especially since Coach Olson had just retired.

It's interesting, when we had this meeting with everyone people were a little reluctant to talk, except for Coach Dunlap. He stood up and looked in each of our eyes for a few seconds. I remember exactly what he told us and this is still in my head. He said "when life throws you a curve ball you can still hit a home run." He mentioned how we were going to be put to the ultimate test and now every single one of us was going to be under a bigger microscope, and it was up to us as a group to come together because we needed each other more than ever. We were this group of thirteen guys berried deep in the trenches and the next six months would show people what type of character we had and the resiliency of each individual on this team.

Coach Olson was the gentleman's coach, the class act of college basketball, the one who gave guys like me a chance to relish the experience of being a walk-on at the most prestigious program on the west coast since John Wooden's UCLA teams of the 1960's and 1970s. He was an ambassador for the game of College basketball. He made people want to play hard and play smart, and play together. He took ordinary players and molded them into extraordinary human beings. It was hard to move on, hard to think about my senior year without him being there. But at the end of the day, we all had to stick together and realize that everything happens for a reason and things like this will only make us stronger in the long run.

When we had practice that day I thought it was going to be a train-wreck. However, it was one of the most efficient practices we had all year. Passing, catching, cutting, shooting, all the good stuff was great for three hours. We had to find a way to relax our minds, get our heart-rates up and fine tune some things that needed to be worked on. In fact, the next several practices were very good. They were on point. I could sense something that wasn't there a few practices before. We were tired, but it was good tired. It was "hey let's come back and do this tomorrow tired."

Initially, when Coach Olson retired, I wanted to quit; there was a moment when my teammates and I sat in the locker room together before one of the many team meetings we were having thinking "Where do we go from here?" I think everyone was thinking about hanging it up or transferring or moving on to something else for six months. I thought about that first conversation I had in his office my freshman year; I was holding onto every word he said and thinking about all the good memories I had with him.

My first thought was making sure that Coach Olson was going to be alright. It didn't matter what others were saying and what the media was saying at the time; my concern was the man's health and how he was doing. I honestly didn't know what was going to happen during the season. I thought the administration might go out and bring in a big named coach to fill the void we had for the initial five to six months of the season. Or we could've had an interim coach; and that's what happened.

Originally we all thought Coach Dunlap was going to take the job but for whatever reason he declined the offer. It was passed down to Coach Pennell. Coach Pennell was a personable guy, he established relationships with the players and again we had another meeting to talk about things. I thought this was good because I think the general public thought we were a group of "downers" and we were going to just mope our way through the season. We had other things in mind though.

When we had all those team meetings and the "player's only meetings", we established this continuity and actually became closer as a group and as teammates. The whole campus was talking about it for weeks leading up to the start of our season; students looked dejected when the news broke all over school, like the world had ended and there was nothing to play for.

The local media were scattered all throughout campus trying to find us and get what they could. If they couldn't find us they were looking for regular students to get their thoughts on the situation. My professors were asking me if I was holding up alright and offered me help whenever I needed it.

During one of our final team meetings before we had our first game, we found out a few things. I thought it was interesting how things were handled after Coach Olson retired. The administration, along with the rest of the school and the city of Tucson, hit the panic button because in their minds, we were in for another up and down season. We were the players and we didn't even hit the panic button; we couldn't, if we did, everything would've became chaos.

There was a genuine fear that set in throughout the atmosphere; it was the first time I'd seen people lose themselves and become caught up in everything. Boosters were coming to the basketball office and our practices every other few days to check in on the state of our team and see how we were going to respond. On the surface certain people treated us great but behind closed doors there was significant doubt and people lost interest in us as a team and as people.

Immediately a panic attack had set in and fans had assumed the worst was going to happen, and this was all before game number one. Part of me wanted to go to the newspaper and media and ask for help from all the fans because we needed everyone more than ever, but I realized that if our team stuck together and took care of business, it didn't matter who was in the stands.

Initially, I thought my senior year was going to be the beginning of a long rebuilding process for our program. All the fans in Tucson were spoiled because of the legacy that Coach Olson had left behind and the way he built the program from ground zero. So when he retired, they thought everything was on a decline, it's natural in a fans eyes because in a basketball crazed city, this is what they live for.

Everyone, including some of us on the team, underestimated our assistant coaches. Part of it was because we didn't know any of them the way we knew Coach Rosborough and Coach Pastner. So when the season came, we had to do everything on the fly. All three assistant coaches could've easily walked away from our team and us but they didn't, they promised us they would stick with us until the day the season ended. That's why everyone will always appreciate what our coaching staff did for us. There was that genuine sense of care that was salt and peppered with tough love and it wound up working out for both parties.

One of the great things about these three assistant coaches was that they had our backs, and it didn't matter what the situation was or what our role was on the team. Each coach had an open door policy and encouraged us to come in as much as we could during the season. The position the coaches were put in was more like a six month project, and my teammates and I were the individuals who needed the help. When we were in "the trenches" during the season I was glad they were on the bench. Right away I noticed these guys didn't miss a beat with anything during practices or games.

Chapter 11

I WAS TOLD ALONG WITH the rest of the guys, that our banquets we usually attended on the road were all of a sudden cancelled. Every year we went to banquets in Phoenix and the bay area and because of our situation they were cancelled. In the administrations minds, as well as outsiders, we were showing up to games with an interim coaching staff, twelve players and no reason for hope, so why would they continue to have banquets for us? Coach Dunlap often made it a point of his to tell us that the only people who cared about our team were in the arena during practice, causing us to take a good, hard look at each other and appreciate what the words family and brotherhood actually meant.

We had to adapt to the coaching style of the interim coaches which took us about a month. Coach Dunlap was definitely the most unique out of the new staff; he brought this mentality with him that rubbed off on a lot of us. During practices if he saw something he didn't like, he made sure that we knew and that his voice was heard. Dunlap would go on these tangents and talk about everything from his own childhood experiences to working Magic Johnson's camps.

I'd never seen anything like this before and I thought I saw it all with Coach O'Neill; he often called our practice facility "the laboratory" and while other teams were having public practices, boasting, and getting all the national attention, we were the silent, diligent team that was trying to perfect our craft and get ready for an intense season.

We hit a bump in the road our second game of the season; we were a young team and we had been through a lot before we started games but I didn't think we'd hit a bump until a few games in.

One of the most humbling experiences we had was playing in the pre-season NIT at the University of Georgia. We lost our game a few days before that would've sent us to New York and this was our reward; playing in front of my teammate Jordan Hill's family in Georgia. There were fewer fans at our games than there were at YMCA gentlemen's leagues.

We were so used to taking chartered flights to all of our games with a strong entourage of fans behind us and we had to share our airplane with another team, who we wound up playing our second game out there in Georgia. It was the first time in my life I could actually hear what I sounded like when I cheered at games. As embarrassing as it may have been, the experience playing in front of virtually no one humbled all of us.

Nobody seemed to care about our team until we shocked the college basketball world and beat Gonzaga up in Phoenix when they were ranked fourth in the country. I always thought how funny it was when we'd win a big game like that and the way fans reacted to it. Weeks before that game against Gonzaga we were left dead in the water and with anything short of a lifeline; people were ready to reel in the next era of Arizona basketball and support us with "moral victories".

All of sudden everyone sees a group of guys that should've gotten ran out of the gym come out and shock the world and finally get some respect. Even my parents and my own best friend thought we were going to be the ones who lost that game. Momentum is a scary thing; create enough of it and everyone tags along, telling you to your face how great you are and how much you mean to the school and city; that is until you make one mistake and then become the talk of the school in a bad way.

That was the one thing that bothered me my senior year more than anything else, fans were almost band-wagon like when we won and then had no problem jumping off of it when we lost a few games here and there. We were informed everyday that our fans were in it for the sprint, not the marathon, which made every game mean that much more to all of us. Games meant a lot to me because I realized that this was the last time I was going to have a road game with my teammates or a non-conference tournament with these guys.

We were a scrappy group of guys, from the top of the team all the way down to me at the end of the bench. The problem was we just weren't very deep. I knew we were a good team when we beat Kansas right before Christmas time. They lost a lot but had still had a stellar group of guys returning; we were the team that had to serve the knockout punch to a group of guys fresh off of winning a national championship.

Our pre-game ritual was something in itself; I'd fire the guys up as much as I can with the time I was given. I became a human pinball in those huddles, getting pushed down and all around. My attitude towards it was simple; I was a senior and the young guys had no idea why I would act crazy during those rituals but it helped. If I could help these guys ready for any type of game then I would be contributing to this team some how.

It hit me in the locker room that I was only three months and some change away from being done with college basketball and onto the next phase of my life. I had seen the different faces come and go every year; whether it was to graduation or early entry for the NBA draft or transfers.

I was allowed to go home for Christmas but I stayed in Tucson because our break was only two days; that's not much of a break for anyone to really do anything. When my parents heard I was staying in Tucson they were livid. They kept asking me how I was going to spend my Christmas break. I told them I had a place to go and enjoy the holiday; in the morning I woke up, wished everyone a Merry Christmas and then snuck into Mckale center later that day and ran sprints on the court and ran the bleachers for a little while before I headed to the Christmas dinner. The place I went to was Denny's the restaurant; the place was empty for the most part, outside of a few families scattered out through the place.

I thought it was nice being alone; at first, part of me wished I was at home with my family but I had some time to reflect on everything; the season, which was supposed to be anything short of a failure started out alright. Being a walk-on I had a lot of time to reflect on things; I often found myself walking campus or eating by myself and contemplating every avenue or way I knew.

That's what college basketball did to guys like me; even as a senior who had been put on scholarship there was still a part of me that always wanted more than what I was getting from the team. I always had that feeling for a few minutes and questioned what life would've been like at a smaller school, being the "go to" guy and being the one who is asked to shoulder the load as oppose to hopping on the shoulders of my teammates, the guys who were brought into score at will and do everything.

I often wondered what it would've been like to have a team full of walk-ons just to see how coaches would've reacted to having a team full of mediocre players and then try to mold them into special talents. That would've been the ultimate joy ride for guys like me who rode the bench for four years; having a team where everyone thinks they're better than they really are.

We were back at practice on December 26th and the looks on everyone's faces were all the same, no one really wanted to be there. That's what happens when we heard the words "time off". Guys have to get back in that mode of doing things under intense circumstances and for some of us it takes longer. I wanted to tell all the guys that I spent my Christmas dinner alone just to see the reactions on my teammates faces but I don't think they would've believed me, they probably would've thought I was doing it for attention or to get a rise out of them.

It was a short and sweet 2 hour practice with a lot of scrimmaging and drill work as usual and now it became fun, pac-10 season. It was looming on everyone's calendars; we were the talk of the league both locally within the conference and nationally. Ever since Coach O retired the main focus was on our team and our coaching staff and how we would respond to all of this.

League play was like the start of a new season. Eighteen games; nine on the road and nine at home, familiar territories and three months to prove to everyone why we were deserving of an invite to the NCAA tournament. After some of those practices when the coaches would use conditioning to prove their points, I was ready for the season to be over with. Towards the end of my time at Arizona my moods ran hot and cold because one day we were clicking as a group and one day we looked like a team full of knuckleheads who didn't deserve to be college basketball players.

That was the frustrating theme that ran through my mind repeatedly; how are we going to go out as a team? The better our team does, the more people will remember all of us as individuals for overcoming adversity and being able to shoulder a load that was beyond heavy.

To start off our road trips I was rooming with DJ Shumpert; he was a freshman at the time and we used to have these talks about everything, from basketball to life. I told him that you start to see your character come out when you become a senior and the season becomes a countdown. It was a "catch 22"; "when the season begins you go through hell, and when it ends, you can see everything within the blink of an eye" I used to tell myself along with my teammates. I told DJ how fortunate I was to be at Arizona and a basketball player; he used to pop that question that would go through my mind vividly before I brought myself back to reality. "Don't you wish you could be out there?" he would say casually.

My sarcastic side wanted to answer him with that look that says "What do you think?" but because he was a freshman and had a lot to learn about everything I used to respond to him by saying "It is what it is". Truth be told, if any of my coaches wanted to throw me in games at any point they would've thrown me in there and tested me to see what I would do during real game time instead of my traditional "walk-on" game time.

Like my former teammate Bret Brielmaier, who was a great player and friend, DJ was a different type of walk-on than I was; he was recruited to come to Arizona so in his mind, he was expecting to hear his number called during important segments of the game. I was that guy who was happy to be here and I carried that label with me through my senior year. I really had no choice, if I showed signs of being bitter or had constant frowns my coaches could've and probably would've asked me to leave.

I told him I understood what he was feeling because to anyone that's recruited it's hard sitting there and watching guys out there in games who you make look bad in practices doing thing you could be doing, but in my case I was used to it from the time I stepped on campus. I never lost sleep over the fact that I had a bunch of "Did Not Play" notes in the stat box. We formed a good friendship and I would tell him to be himself and continue to work hard and somehow things would work out for him.

We started off at the bay area and in between games we attended this function called the bay-cats banquet and it is a banquet for all the people who are affiliated with the University of Arizona who are from the bay area. I went with Coach Pennell and I got to speak. It was a great experience, the networking, the people I met, the food, and of course, I got to build up Coach Pennell and show off my public speaking skills. Personally I loved these banquets, it's another opportunity we all get to meet new people and I love doing that, it took up an hour or so but it was worth it. Those banquets were routine for me to speak at; it was part of my title of being a walk-on and having that asterisk next to my name.

Before the start of the second semester I went out with some friends to a bar. We had just had our first two home games of league play; technically we weren't supposed to go out during the season, and especially the day before school started, but it was my last semester and school and I felt like I deserved at least one mulligan; I sacrificed so much on Saturday nights during my first three years, often shooting and working out by myself while other guys were going out and doing typical things college fraternity guys do.

While I was there all I could focus on was wanting to be in the practice facility working out. That's how annul I became about putting in work and not being able to go out and have a good time. Constantly looking over my shoulder and wondering whether or not I'd be there the next day created that sense of urgency and made me want to work even harder and do things that other people wouldn't want to do when it was time to have fun.

As league play continued every week, we were struggling to find our identity as a team. I loved when coaches threw that pitch my way and asked that question "who are we?" I would look around and think to myself we were a group of guys who honestly didn't' want to be there after Coach Olson retired but we weren't going to give in that easily like most of us expected. Just because we weren't going to give up didn't mean we were guaranteed wins and it certainly didn't mean our opponents were going to feel sorry or take it easy on us.

If anything, teams started gunning for us even more during league play to try to get us to give up and sink down low to a level that only bad teams knew of. The more we lost, the more all of us suffered, whether it was in practice, in our classes, or socially. It's not fun taking several days to prepare for an opponent and then guys don't come ready to play.

Halfway through the season I changed roommates on the road; initially I was paired up with DJ Shumpert but was later switched to room with Jordan Hill. Jordan was different, to say the least. We didn't have that much in common outside of basketball and like my former teammate Marcus Williams, the better he played, the bigger his head grew and the more invincible he thought he became.

In our hotel room it was often Jordan's way or the highway. Jordan was a guy that used his size, his personality, and his look, to his advantage. We were two people from completely different ends of the spectrum. He never talked to me unless he was discussing a girl he had coming into the room that night or something he was putting in his car. He was 6 '10 and grew out his hair over the three years we were teammates to have dreadlocks. His arms were covered in tattoos, all of them which had important meaning; and his personality was a combination of an overgrown kid with bully-like instincts, who knew he could get away with anything he wanted to on our team because he was the only true big guy we had my senior year.

He didn't care that we had a big game the next day; he was more concerned with what girl was coming into the room and how good she looked. When I would go down to quiet rooms in hotels to get homework done, Jordan often told me to go "fetch" him some snacks, usually it was candy and soda. The few times I said no to this guy caused him to wrestle with me in our hotel room just to prove his point.

Of course when I came back with the candy and soda, that I paid for with my perdium money, he was all smiles and said the typical pacifying line, telling me what a great teammate and friend I was and there was nobody else on this team like me, and this was all before the night time rolled around in the hotel room.

If I were in Jordan's position as a player, I would've never thought twice about having females in the hotel room, or doing half the stuff he did. But I wasn't, I was a walk-on whose margin for error was slim and none compared to a guy like Jordan. He was a future pro who had the most upside in the draft, according to some analysts and experts that cover college basketball. So in his mind, he had become college basketball royalty overnight. When you're constantly referred to as being part of a group that's known as "The big three", I guess it gets to your head sooner or later.

When the night time rolled around on the road in our hotel room, Jordan often told me in advance, usually discreetly at a team meal, if he had a girl coming in that night. I kept quiet every time, even though I shouldn't have. There was a fine line between being a good teammate and doing the right thing, or as other people would've put it – being a rat. I had to play the roll of the walk-on sidekick by letting the girls in the room and then covering for him the next morning at our team breakfast meals because he was usually sitting on certain hours of sleep you could count on one hand. I felt like the coaches knew, or at least had an idea of what was going on to some degree.

I dreaded walking into those team meals the morning after; Jordan often held us up because he knew he could; and when we got into our meeting room to watch film and eat, all sets of eyes were directed towards the two of us. I used to think if the coaches caught Jordan for breaking a team rule on the road, they would've sent me home instead.

When we would get back to Tucson after road trips, I would tell him in our team vans as we were being transported back to the arena that I couldn't cover for him for that much longer. He never cared to hear it because that's just how his mind worked; other guys looked at me like I was crazy for bringing it up but I just never wanted to get in trouble, but because I was a walk-on, that's how my mind worked; I was concerned for my teammates even though some of them weren't concerned about me.

When we were in Los Angeles playing USC I got to see my parents after our game. We went to dinner and my dad took me back to that question, asking me "What have you learned from the experience?" He kept telling me to soak everything in because within the blink of an eye graduation will be coming and then the real world would be up next. I wanted to tell him what I saw with my own two eyes, but I often sugar coated things because I didn't want my parents to hit the panic button knowing what a walk-on really goes through every day.

It's hard to hide the emotions that I felt sometimes with everything that I took from my teammates, but a smile on the outside sometimes shields what is really happening on the inside and it got to the point that days were going by so fast and there was so much happening things started to go one ear and out the other.

When we lost to Arizona State, our rival school, students and fans lost complete confidence in us. It was the story everyone was waiting for, a group of guys teetering one game at a time which would lead to chaos within the program. In one fell swoop we all became the laughing stock of campus, causing people to shake their heads constantly and making me contemplate whether or not I should show my face on campus.

It's one thing to be a walk-on for the basketball team; everyone knows I don't play unless the game is over but to be a walk-on for a team that's struggling and having an identity crisis is embarrassing. When we were losing games I wanted to go up to a normal student and ask if I could trade places for a day just so I could be an outsider looking in and have some sense of normality in my life.

As a group we had hit rock bottom in a sense, I felt like it didn't matter what we did. It didn't matter how much film we watched or how thick the scouting reports were for the upcoming opponents, I could see in everyone, even myself that the moral of our team was down and people were ready to give up on us; except our coaching staff. Coach Pennell called us into a huddle one day and told us how much basketball was left to be played and reminded us how scary momentum was.

I thought if we got enough of it on our side we might be able to muster up something and have a shot at the Tournament. We needed to catch a break though.

I always thought luck was when preparation meets opportunity. But what happened on January 24th, 2009 was something that I think everyone from our team will remember for the rest of our lives. I always remember seeing those epic comebacks when teams were down by double digit points in the final seconds of a game and they find some way to win. I had never been a part of that but always thought it was pretty cool if I had been. The bottom line was we needed a win and we needed it bad.

These boys jumped on us hitting three after three after three point shot. We hit ours too but we weren't going to win exchanging baskets with them. We had to lock their asses up on the defensive end. We had dug ourselves in a hole and with fifty seconds left we were down ten points. That's an awfully difficult obstacle for a team who's supposed to throw in the towel and give up. I don't care what anyone says a ten point lead with fifty seconds left usually means the game is over and in the refrigerator. But something happened that really changed our season during that game.

When chase took a charge in one of the plays was a foul and he and one of Houston's players Aubrey Coleman got tangled up. Aubrey Coleman got up first and started to walk back to the play, but as he walked over to the play he stepped on Chases face. This, by far, was one of the craziest things I had ever seen, I thought the game was over, so did the rest of our crowd as they got up and left. But when that happened and I saw Chase get up I saw something I had never seen in him before. I saw this fire that was lit in him and almost this anger that came right out of left field. Chase has always been pretty laidback and that was really the turning point in our season, that fire and passion motivated everyone else and ignited an even bigger fire. I remember when he came back to the huddle he was so upset, he had this look in his eyes like he wasn't going to be denied and if you wanted something you had to take it from him.

We made a few shots in the final fifty seconds, called all the right timeouts, ran our pressing defense great, and forced them into overtime. It was crazy because all the fans that walked out on us were trying to get back into the arena and watch the game. Mckale center became a mad-house and now a game between two unranked opponents turned into the game of the week with an epic comeback made for ESPN Classic.

We won the game in overtime and when we got to the locker room we all had this look on our faces like "what the hell just happened?" To this day I still talk about it with my friends and we all agree that the game against Houston was the game that saved our season. The basketball Gods had seen us bleeding for the last month or so and realized that we needed a break and we finally caught it.

Within hours the whole town decided to rally around us after our team pulled off a miracle over Houston. We reeled off seven consecutive wins and started to regain the confidence that escaped us during the beginning of league play. Like I had seen in the past, there was a legitimate buzz that was created with every game approaching during this winning streak.

As a team we were on cloud nine; but we had to be careful because whenever a young group like ours has overnight success, most people think that they arrive and it can always come back to hurt you in the end. At one point ESPN's analysts were saying we were one of the hottest teams in the nation and we had played our way back into the tournament. I thought that we were a tournament team all along we just caught a few bad breaks, now that we had some momentum we had to do everything we could to keep it going for as long as we could.

The bandwagon was immediately being hopped back onto by our fans, our students, and college basketball "experts" all over the country. I thought we were so hot we weren't going to lose again until we got to postseason play. I always believed when we'd lose games or go on losing streaks of three games or more, we'd lose relationships with fans and our students until we pulled off a win and pacified them with a few wins here and there.

During another team meeting, Coach Penne and the staff told us not to get to ahead of ourselves because there was a lot of basketball left to be played and we were the team everybody was gunning for. I thought that's how it was from the beginning of the season, everybody wanted a shot at Arizona without their head coach, but now that this team was winning and gaining ground on everyone, it created an even bigger bull's eye on our backs.

The ironic thing about this winning streak was that during this particular time period when we won those seven games, we had no official leader on the team. We had captains that we voted for; but that doesn't mean we had genuine leaders. I tried to lead but according to my teammates and some eyes of the public, a walk-on can't be the leader on a team from the bench. Our coaching staff was our true leader at the time. Those trenches became worthwhile when we were winning because the coaches were leading the way through the trenches with their hard hats, flashlights, and clip boards; and we were piggy backing on everything they did.

Coach Dunlap continued to challenge us to find leadership from any avenue, stressing the importance of leadership on a young team like ours during crucial points of the season. Often calling us out at practices telling us how much we needed to come together in order to keep the momentum going.

We carried our seven game winning streak into Tempe as we were geared up to play Arizona State again. Both parties knew what was at stake and the importance of the game. Ironically we were playing our rival school in the biggest game of the season; they didn't like us and we didn't like them. The arena was jam-packed and all I could hear were people bashing us from left to right; I almost wanted to put in some ear plugs in so I could focus on the games, but I knew since I wasn't going to play that much I could observe the crowd and try to get a feel for the atmosphere.

Having a winning streak snapped is frustrating because we felt invincible for those few weeks, feeling like we were incapable of fault, and then within forty minutes of the confines of college basketball it was taken from us by a group of arrogant players who were well coached.

In the bigger scheme of things, it was one game, but because we had struggled so much during the beginning of the season, losing one game had more consequences for us than for the regular opponent.

In the locker room it was back to that familiar scene, heads down, towels over faces, all of us, myself included, with an uncertain look on our faces not knowing how to grasp a loss. As a team we had this moment in the locker room when it was us and the silence; Coach Dunlap asked "The big three" which consisted of Chase, Jordan and Nic what their goals for this team were. Jordan and Nic said for us to make the tournament. Chase said for us to get out of the first weekend of the tournament and make some sort of a run because he thought we were capable. When he said that everyone kind of looked around at each other and there was a look on our faces and we all thought we could do it but there was little spec of doubt that still lingered.

Coach Dunlap didn't ask any of us "other guys" what are goals for the season where. I had to ask myself internally what my goal was. Obviously, given the circumstances we'd been through as a team, making the NCAA tournament would've been good enough for everyone to live with. I knew we could do more than just make the tournament though; if we were fortunate to get back that momentum we had during our seven game joy-ride than we could actually make some noise.

As a group, we had a loss hangover, and we carried with us everywhere; it festered into our everyday life even though people were still riding our bandwagon. Now our whole team was going to be tested during this last stand of games we were about to face. I tried to be as encouraging as I could during crucial parts of the season but when a group like ours went down we didn't just become down, we became down and out.

Our season took an interesting turn when we were in Washington and our whole team had to design the practice schedule; it seemed easy but it was surprisingly difficult, I had my first glimpse of what coaches actually go through when they put their time into a practice schedule that's supposed to prepare all of us for a game. The schedule we designed wound up being a team film session of us breaking down the opponent while the coaches stayed quiet. To me, I felt like I had the keys to the car in a sense, for the first time as a basketball player, I was able to tell my teammates what they were doing wrong and they would have to sit there, listen, and listen hard.

They couldn't stand up and tell me to get lost, this was a real film session put on by all of us players and in this case, Coach Pennell and his staff were the brains behind the scenes for the idea of the session. I always thought if I had been able to do that from day one it would've changed a lot of things. Being on the bench for all but thirty seconds during games, I saw things that players didn't see when they were out on the floor. It was the best seat in the house without paying, just a lot of sacrifice.

We lost momentum when we finished our last stand of road games and now we became in a situation where it was "do or die", for everyone; it was hard to fathom. That question my father asked me as I entered my senior year started to loom over my head again. The way we played during our last handful of games was atrocious. I didn't think we deserved to make the postseason unless we found a way to win. If I was a member of the team that broke that tournament streak Coach Olson had established with previous teams, I wouldn't want to show my face around campus anymore.

During a lot of our home games my senior year, especially league play, I often looked directly across the arena and about four rows up; because that's where Coach Olson was sitting. He often sat there with his family or his close friends; observing and taking the games by his own account.

Even during our huddles I would occasionally glance my head over and see him stand up and shifting his eyes on us while other fans were talking; I used to wonder what would happen if he came over, pushed everyone out of the way and took over the clipboard and started coaching us to a victory.

That would've been the ultimate experience and comeback, but Coach Olson was sitting behind the sidelines and that meant he was sitting back while another Coach was taking the reins and sitting in the same chair he used to sit in. Part of me could tell he was itching to get back out there and coach but he also wanted to watch the games without being disturbed.

Before my last two home games my senior year I snuck out of my house late one night, went to get some extra shooting in, and then stood at half court at our arena, the McKale Center. My feet were on the center circle of half court that read "Lute and Bobby Olson Court" and I was going back and forth between sitting down and standing and my movement was continuous for several minutes.

Four years is a long time to be involved with something; even in my case, being that guy that doesn't play but comes back for more, and not knowing what the next day holds and living a life of uncertainty, wanting a shot, and occasionally looking over my shoulder to make sure I'm not getting cut. Every day, and night, this arena, filled with different locker rooms, a training room, a weight room, study areas, staff members and hundreds of student-athletes from all over the world, was a place that I often called home.

When the bleachers were out and all fifteen thousand seats were out in front of me I looked around and realized I had the best audience watching me, absolutely nobody. That made this particular moment in the arena more pleasant. I started this journey here at Arizona by myself, decided to put in extra work frequently, by myself, and I stood on the half court center circle a few nights before my senior night game, by myself.

I found it hard to believe that I was so close to being done with college basketball and college. I didn't want to say goodbye to the crowd in the arena that opened their arms to me when I came in as a wide-eyed Freshman who was "happy to be here", all the way to my senior year, when I tried to emerge into something of a vocal leader on a team that was doubted by virtually everyone outside of ourselves and coaches.

During that week leading up to the games, our school newspaper wrote an article on me; it was called "The Legend of David Bagga." It was about my journey and saying I had come so far from being a walk-on to where I am now and how I am a very team oriented guy and I do whatever I can to fire my teammates up before games. It was almost a feel-good story for people to read because the funny thing was that people around campus knew that I was a walk-on but they didn't really know my story and how I made the team and what my journey was like. I never thought of myself the way the paper portrayed me to be, I just felt blessed that people appreciated an underappreciated walk-on who wanted nothing but the best for his teammates when his teammates were going to battle.

My parents called and said how proud they were of me and my mom started joking with me saying how I was this legend on and off the court. The conversation also triggered my father to ask that question about my experience as a walk-on. My best friend Mitch called and he told me that heroes get remembered but legends never die. It's a line from the movie "The Sandlot." And my teammates and coaches said how proud they were of me, that meant a lot to me because it made me realize that even if you don't get all the playing time in the world you can still have an impact on your team somehow and by being there for your teammates and pushing them in practice the end result can be very rewarding.

March 7th, 2009; the day I will remember for the rest of my life. For as long as I can remember, I always wanted to be that guy that hit the big shot and made the fans stand up, take notice, and say they remembered me for something phenomenal; not just for being that guy who was often spotted going crazy cheering for his teammates. The way our season was unfolding, none of us knew what was going to happen as we headed into our conference tournament. All I knew was that, I had put in this time for four years, busting my tail and sacrificing everything from my spare time to my body and because of this I was going to receive a special day which is known as "Senior Day".

There's a lot to be said for senior day; I looked back at everything leading up to the game and the day. I didn't think I was going to make it to this point and even as the game approached, I was even surprised at myself that I appeared to make it, somewhat unscathed. Even during our practice and our team meal, my mind was in a completely different place than with the guys. My mind had wondered back to that empty arena that consumed me for four long years, my home, and it was telling me that for one last home game, I get to put on an Arizona Jersey and cheer for my teammates as loud as I could, be the guy that Coach Olson said for me to be from day one, and hope to add to the journey that I embarked on when I was a freshman.

It was special to me because my parents were also in town and they had only been to three total games, all of them were on the road. While it was the last home game for me, ironically for my parents, it was their first home game they would watch. I was on the phone with my mom and she kept asking me all sorts of questions about the game, the team, the coaches, and everything in-between. My mom kept asking me how loud McKale Center got during our games and

I told her it would get pretty loud. I also told her that when we were winning by a large amount, it got even louder. It went from loud to extreme, and she kept asking me why. I kept telling her you'll have to see it for yourself to understand. It was difficult for me to tell my parents that the reason the arena got so loud was because they were chanting my name to go in.

The night before the game, I roomed with Zane Johnson, a sophomore at the time, and like I had done previous times with other roommates, I was up all night. My adrenaline was going at a hundred miles per hour and we were still a whole day away from game time.

Zane kept asking me what I was feeling inside and how I was dealing with this being my last game to a long journey that was eventually coming to an end. He kept telling me I was going to go in and score and people were going to go crazy the same way I go crazy on the bench when my teammates score. All I could do was laugh, I tried to cover up my emotions by telling him how focused I was for the game, when secretly I wanted to tell him how great it would be have a senior day like no one had before and go out like a champion.

I didn't need to be focused; unless the clock was at forty seconds and we were up by a lot, there was no reason for me to be focused. I knew that it didn't matter if I were a walk-on or an All-American; if we won the last home game people would remember it, for reasons of their own. He was telling me in our shoot-around and in our pre-game meal that something good was going to happen. I was trying to visualize something great and it was almost as if Zane knew something was coming my way.

I prepared for the game like I would any other home game; arriving several hours prior to game time and get an early workout in and then relax in the locker room until it was time to go out and shoot with the other guards. When I was by myself in the arena before the game, I almost broke down and started crying, not because there was something wrong, but I just wished that the journey of being an Arizona Wildcat didn't have to end. It didn't matter to me that I had been hit by teammates, picked on at practice or even left out of drills over the years, I would've been a college basketball player for the next twenty years if I had the opportunity to do so.

The arena was crammed with breathing room only; there were fans that were in red all over the place. My eyes were shifting back and forth, from the action of the game, all the way up to where my parents were sitting back down to where Coach Olson was sitting. It was a triangle of important people who were there in attendance which made the day even more special.

Patiently I sat there, next to the end of the bench and our trainer with that towel around my neck; my shoes were tied unusually tight and my body was filled with adrenaline and emotions that were riding higher than ever. The crowd rallied behind us from the beginning, sensing we were hurting and in desperation for a win to get that precious momentum back and give us a ray of hope to make the NCAA Tournament. Every second of every minute ticked down quicker and before I knew it, we were at the tail end of the game.

My time, like my journey, was running out for me to even go in and touch the ball, let alone get in and shoot the basketball in front of my family; it was my last chance as a senior to do something out there. Luckily for me, those basketball Gods were on my side again, and with twenty-five valuable seconds remaining, I would have my chance to get in the game in front of our home crowd, my teammates, and my parents, one last time.

Slowly, starters and the guys in the rotation were making their way to the bench; I was sitting there in a calm fashion and the mood of the arena had shifted and gotten quiet. Coach Pennell looked at me, gave me the nod, and then came over to the end of the bench and gave me an initial push to the scorers table.

As I made my way to the scorers table to check into the game, the arena went from quiet to loud and fans were showing the support they showed me throughout my four years there as a walk-on. Students had signs; friends pointed and yelled random phrases to me. Most of them were telling me to shoot the basketball. My parents sat a few rows up behind the basket, and like myself, they were soaking every second of the moment in.

Chase came up to me and the initial plan was for me to sag back so I could get a dunk and go out in style. I wanted to shoot a three point shot because that's what I'd always done; check into the game, catch and shoot, hope the ball goes through the basket, and then go home, it became routine. It was almost as if God heard my request and gave me an opportunity to catch a break for being a walk-on.

When I got in the game Nic was at the free throw line and he made his second free throw to give us ninety-eight points. When the player for Stanford threw the ball in bounds, the ball he made a mistake and threw the ball away; Nic grabbed it and that's when it happened.

I came up behind Nic, and the crowd came up behind me, creating a buzz before I even touched the basketball. Nic, being the unselfish person that he was, threw me what's called a shovel pass and then I took it from there. As the ball left my hands and my unorthodox shooting form, I initially thought the attempt was going to miss but it would be a "good effort". But as it kept traveling further down and made its way to the basket, I knew it was going in.

The arena went from loud to chaotic; the eruption from the crowd was almost volcanic. I saluted the student section, along with the rest of the crowd because if it wasn't for them, I may have never had a chance to have gone in and prove I belonged. In a way, they persuaded my coaches to put me in and give me that chance. It was my way of saying thank you; they helped send an unlikely basketball player out, who wasn't supposed to be in there to begin with. I couldn't hear myself breathe, let alone talk; even I couldn't believe what had just happened, and I was the guy that hit the shot. I sat around on the bench for two plus hours and then came in pulled a trigger of hope and thankfully it went in.

I kept thinking all those long nights shooting deep three point shots by myself in the arena finally paid off, to a certain degree. It wasn't a game winning shot but a journey winning shot; there really was no better way to go out, especially on my senior day. Since I was a freshman I had seen my senior teammates lose their last home game and I didn't want to be one of those guys looking back with that look on my face knowing what could've been.

The clock hit triple zero's all around and the arena stayed on their feet for several minutes after the buzzer sounded. My parents were there smiling, my mom was crying out of joy, not believing what she had just seen. My teammates ran to me as quick as they could, ambushed me at the scene and shared the moment with me and we all celebrated like we had won the national championship. Fans were crying, some of them saying they had never heard the arena that loud in numerous years. I found it ironic the crowd was cheering for a guy who wasn't supposed to be out there.

After the game, I was presented with my jersey, it was framed in a glass case and I held it up to the crowd, who applauded. I did something as a tribute to Coach Olson. I kissed Lute and Bobby Olson Court. It was his name that was on the middle of the half court and I knew it was something I wanted to do. It didn't matter whether we won or lost, I wanted to pay my respect to the man who gave me the opportunity to play in college. As soon as I kissed the court, I turned, looked at Coach Olson and pointed to him and said thank you; he nodded and smiled at me.

The only thing that was missing from my senior day ceremony was Coach Olson being there on the court to present me with my jersey in that hard case. I thought it was ironic when I received my jersey from Coach Pennell because I was a walk-on and he was an interim coach. Two guys, who had taken positions that weren't going to last very long; being a walk-on was almost like having an interim position because at some point it had to end for both of us and we would move onto other opportunities.

Later that night my family and I went out to dinner and there were about forty students there, most of them from the game. I walked in with my parents and my brother and I sat down to order some food and as I ordered from our waiter, the students all throughout the restaurant started chanting my name for about ten minutes. People were so nice and so warm and caring it was great to be a part of it.

That game was my reward from everything I had endured as a walk-on, the times I had been made fun of or told I didn't belong and within the blink of an eye, everyone saw that I did belong. After I left the restaurant I went home, sat on my bed, and just looked at my jersey in the glass case for a few hours, thinking how much it meant to me that I was fortunate to have a moment like this.

My best friend Mitch called me and told me to turn on the television because I made ESPN; I didn't believe him until I actually saw it. I was wondering what all the doubters back home were thinking when they were watching their television sets that night.

I walked campus a few days after and there was still a buzz that had been created because of the shot that I hit. Students were coming up, talking to me, shaking my hand, and treating me like a hero, all because that shot went in the basket. I had wondered how I would've been treated if I missed the shot or never even attempted the shot. Would there still be that same amount of caring?

Secretly, there was a part of me thinking it would've been great if the journey ended there, but there was still a lot left we had to do. There was pressure on us as a group to make the tournament, and because we ran into some obstacles the last couple of games everything was up for grabs. It came to the point now that it was a one game season.

The fact that the pac10 tournament was here also meant that the journey itself was almost over; we'd come closer together throughout the year and found out things about ourselves that we didn't even know. It became do or die for our team and we had been put in this situation that was going to put us to the test.

I didn't know what to think during the game, I knew if we won we were going to be a lock for the tournament but if we lost, then the great debate would've taken place about our team, our coach, and our status as a tournament team. During our stay at the hotel, fans from other schools were coming up to me and telling me they saw my senior night game and saying how it was a great way to go out. I didn't think other fans would've done something like that, it caught me off guard.

As a team I don't think we appreciated the opportunity we had in front of us. I felt like my teammates took the approach to the game that I initially had as a walk-on; just happy to be here instead of having the opportunity to step on someone's throat. Arizona State came to play and we didn't, there's really no other way to explain it. Coach Olson was at our game too, I kept looking at him during our timeouts and huddles. He didn't look to happy with what he was seeing, not too many people in the arena did.

We went from being one of the last teams into the tournament to being the last team out. It's frustrating because we had that streak for making the tournament and it was at twenty-four years. Was it over? Were we going to be the team that broke the streak? I sure as hell didn't want that to happen because the way it was looking that was going to be our legacy. The team with all that potential but couldn't muster up enough wins to get to the NCAA Tournament. We were a team that was up and down the whole year and now it became a waiting game and we would soon see where our body of work would take us.

Our fate would be decided by God, and the members of the tournament committee. That was the longest two days of my life; it was so hard to watch all these other teams who had worse records than us win their conference tournaments. I remember I couldn't eat or sleep the first night. I didn't want people to remember our team for being the team that broke the streak that all the previous teams had worked so hard for. It was looking like that before selection Sunday. I called my parents and asked for their opinion and they were honest with me and they felt like we blew a lot of opportunities that were put in front of us this year.

When I walked to class that Friday all the talk was about how we had absolutely no chance of making the tournament and how the team would be even worse next year. I had my headphones on so I didn't hear too much what people had to say about our team or myself. As I walked into class people knew that the energy had been sucked away from our team, I tried just not to think about anything except getting through the day. We had two days off from practice with a couple team meetings sprinkled in here and there.

Even though we were considered a long-shot to make the tournament, the morale was still high on the team. Guys, including myself just wanted to play. I didn't want to end my senior season on that note, losing to a school with no class in a conference tournament.

If we didn't' make the tournament we could either accept a bid to play in the NIT or we could fold up the season and go home for spring break. I felt like there were a lot of mixed feelings from everyone because most of us felt like it would be embarrassing to not be in the NCAA Tournament but at the same time this is a team full of competitors. We had to take a team vote on it but at the end of the day we decided that the NIT would be plan b.

When selection Sunday came we had a team practice for ninety minutes but it was a dry practice with no contact. We just got shots up, ran drills, and did some extra conditioning. It was all business and the practice flew by quicker than usual, with guys contemplating what was going to happen to our team as the minutes came and went. We had a team meal afterwards and all eyes were naturally glued to the television to see what the analysts were saying about us being in the tournament. I turned off my cell phone just because I didn't want to be distracted with everything that was going on and I didn't want to hear what the doubters had to say.

I had to stay as positive and upbeat during the whole two days; it was frustrating hearing negative rumblings from all ends of the spectrum. Obviously I thought we deserved to be in the tournament but it wasn't up to me to decide that, that's why they have the tournament committee. The show started and we sat there as a team like we had done all year and waited patiently. Our fate was about to take a turn to a different road.

Selection Sunday is one of the most unusual days out of the year for college basketball. Some teams get screwed over; some teams get their big break and punch a ticket to the big dance. Being a part of the University of Arizona I never really sweated watching the show, until this year. We had a pretty good deal after practice. As a team we sat there eating together, looking together, and anticipating what was going to happen.

So many questions were being asked in everyone's minds. Our coaching staff had done a great job all year long and we really couldn't have done some of the things without them. Patiently we sat there biting at the bullet to see what was going to happen. As the show started I could see the sweat on guys faces trickle down faster and faster, there was so much adrenaline in the room and we hadn't even been playing a game or anything, we had just been sitting there waiting. Sitting there together as a team, were like a group of little ducks swimming in a lake; on the surface, everything looks calm and content, but underneath and on the inside, everything was going a hundred miles per hour. Every second felt like an hour and then as the announcers starting saying the names of teams that were getting invited to the tournament, the most unlikely name was called; and that's when it happened.

As the selection show approached the Midwest region with the Friday/Sunday games we were one of the first teams to hear our names called. I could remember Greg Gumble's voice saying those words over and over and over again: "Utah vs. Arizona in Miami, Florida." Pandemonium broke out in the tiny conference room we were all in as a team. The mood immediately shifted from fear to fun. It was almost like someone had played a joke on us as a team and then gave us the ultimate surprise by saying our team had made the NCAA Tournament. I had turned my cell phone off and when I turned it back on I had almost 10 voice messages and about 15 missed calls. There it was, we caught it and it fell right into our laps. Our reward? Going to the big dance and erasing any doubt that people had about our team. It was up to all of us to write the rest of this chapter for the 2008-09 Arizona basketball season.

It felt like we were a team that was reborn and on a mission to do something impossible. But isn't that what it's all about? When you have a team like our team and who was up and down all year long and now to finally catch the break that we did it really says a lot; anything's possible. Now we had to go into Miami and beat the odds. A lot of people thought our team didn't belong in the tournament, much like people thought I didn't belong on the team, as a walk-on. The irony was uncanny; I could sense the guys were beginning to feel how I felt throughout four years.

Throughout this whole week of preparation for the tournament I saw something that I hadn't really seen throughout the year; guys were smiling with each other and it really felt like we had this new lease on life. We didn't have that a month prior to where we were at. But, one day can change everything. After our practices we would sit in the locker room and we were all smiles; my teammates and I still couldn't believe what had happened. I was thinking how great it would've been to make something of a run while we here. Realistically a lot of people thought we would lose our first or second game due to our seeding, but we knew all that doubt didn't mean a thing compared to our own belief.

When that plane pulled around into the airport and we boarded in our white jumpsuits we were going with a purpose. Our purpose was to win and to win for ourselves. The coaching staff had instilled this "Us against the world" mentality since the day we started this journey and now it was our job to use that mentality to prove everyone wrong.

This was one of those few times we watched a great deal of film on our opponent. When I say great deal I'm talking about having film sessions plus watching film on our own. There was so much more at stake now, the bar had been raised and everything became a 1 game season and now it was time for everyone and their mom to see what Arizona Basketball was really all about. I was even watching extra film and I didn't even play that much. That's how serious this was to all of us. We were getting the short end of the stick all year long from everybody. So many people had doubted us and now it was our turn, the ball was in our court and it was our move.

One of the best things about the tournament is having a public practice in front of the media. There are so many random people that show up to the arena and it's so easily to get distracted while you're there. It was great though, the whole atmosphere was great. I was just ready and anxious to get this game going. I had adrenaline built up for no apparent reason but I just wanted to get out there and get it going.

I couldn't sleep the night before the game. I was rooming with Jordan Hill on the road and we stayed up for a while talking. For the most part it was about the game coming up but we were just so excited and full of energy we felt like we were ready to get on the court right now. It was one of the few times when we actually conversed and he gave me the time of day. I wanted to get in his head and figure him out as much as I could but the guy was so caught up in his own world; it was tough to get through to the guy unless he wanted me to make the occasional trip to the hotel gift shop to get him candy and soda.

I never told him how mad it made me when he would make me run those errands for him. But this was the tournament and I tried to be as good as a teammate as I could, even for a guy that for the most part, wasn't a good teammate and focused solely on himself.

Coach Dunlap used to reiterate to me that a good teammate goes a long way in the end.

Our shoot-around was all business but it was really our last chance to go over the main points of what we needed to cover before we played Utah. Everyone was on point but that still didn't stop our coaches from yelling at us and being intense. This was our last chance and it could be potentially be our last game if we weren't on point.

There were so many doubters out there that were rooting against us in some way, shape, or form. All we could do was just win, which would silence everyone. Winning really is the only way to silence people, it literally shuts up the nay-Sayers

I remember getting off the bus and walking into the arena, there was a surreal feeling walking in and just knowing what was in front of us was crazy. Another opportunity was waiting for us and it was right there for us to grab onto it.

I was watching all of the coaches and their demeanors in the locker room. It's interesting because nobody was in panic mode and nobody was nervous. If anything, we all were anxious to get out there and get it going. The calmest one was by far Coach Dunlap. He had his folder in one hand with his notes in the other breaking down the personnel of Utah. He began to write things on the board for us to remember throughout the game. All of us were stretching before we could get out there and warm-up. I was sweating so hard before it was even time to go out there just because of the atmosphere because after-all this was the tournament and anything's possible.

Our warm-up was all business. It was quiet but intense, short but productive. Players from Utah were looking down at our end constantly and it was almost as if they were afraid to some extent, like they knew they had ran into a group of hungry predators looking for someone to feast on. Everyone was full of adrenaline and half our team was in familiar territory while half our team was in unsheltered waters, wondering what was going to happen next.

I told the guys in the huddle our time was now; trying to motivate them in some way possible because we weren't going to receive very much kudos from anyone outside of our family. They played rough, we played rougher, they ran their offense hard, we ran ours harder, they made quick cuts, we made our cuts quicker, and we put it all together at the most crucial time of the year.

To everyone's surprise we won the game; the way the game was going I thought it was going to be a pretty big route and I would actually have a chance to get in and play. After we shook hands with the players of Utah we all walked back to the locker room together. There was a lot of silence until we got back to the locker room when we all loosened up, cracked a few smiles, and let out a few screams.

We were all like kids in a candy store, the way we were smiling and cheering and high-fiving each other constantly. My voice was gone from yelling so loud but I didn't care, we had not won a game in the tournament since I was a freshman and the feeling around the locker room was great.

The media had flocked to us like groupies, and the best part about the session was that every single reporter in there looked stunned that we weren't only in the tournament but that we had pulled off the first big shock and beaten a higher seed to advance. In a lot of people's eyes this would be good enough to call our season a success; just making the tournament would've been a success, but there was noise we wanted to make and we had another opportunity to do so.

Back at the hotel we were greeted by our fans and players families; I often wondered what went through everyone's heads when we were coming through that lobby. We had to keep ourselves calm and not think anything of it because it was such a quick turnaround and there was still much work to be done.

We found out that night we'd be playing Cleveland State. They had shocked college basketball by beating Wake Forest in their first round game. I don't know how many people's brackets we messed up but I'm willing to bet it was quite a few.

Our work was cut out for us and the opportunities were coming at will; win and we go to the sweet sixteen, lose and we go home and our season is done. We could control our own destiny but it's like our coaching staff told us throughout the year; our margin of error was very slim compared to most teams, so we had to make sure we were on point again.

We had less than twenty-four hours to prepare for Cleveland State. This wasn't a bad team either, earlier in the year they had beaten Syracuse and made a name for themselves, so we had our work cut out for us. The mood at our team meals was positive; everyone was beaming but tried not to give away their poker faces, food tastes a lot better when you win; you get another lifeline and you get to live and play another day.

Our practice was light but detailed, it required all of us to be there mentally more than physically but there was still a lot we got done. For the guys who didn't play like me we got extra conditioning in as well as more drills. Since it was the tournament they took it easy on me, there was no turning back now, and it was fun having another practice in that arena to get a better feel for the bright lights and the big stage.

There was a lot of downtime back at the hotel so I just caught up on sleep and worked out. That night in our hotel room Jordan and I were talking again before we both went to sleep. We were also watching film of the Utah game and relaxing our minds. I kept asking Jordan what he was feeling out there when he threw down monstrous dunks and making big plays. He didn't say too much at first until I started engaging him with more serious questions about his future. Our conversation then shifted to the NBA, and I kept asking him if he was exited to get paid.

That guy was on his way to making a bundle of money. Everyone knew he was going to be a professional so naturally people wanted to hop on his band wagon. I still didn't know the guy very well; obviously we were teammates for three years but the most we had conversed was when he ordered me to get snacks for him in the hotel gift shop so I tried to take an opportunity to get to know him.

Our conversation then shifted to talking about life and what it would mean to win and go to the sweet sixteen. I told Jordan that if we were to win we would prove a lot of people wrong and do something that everyone would remember for a very long time.

That was something that was on both of our minds because even though he was a future pro and I was a walk-on at the end of the bench, we had both been doing that our whole lives. Nobody ever expected Jordan Hill to play professionally at first because when he came into Arizona in 2006 he was so raw and still learning the game. And no one certainly expected me to be a division one basketball player and who would later earn a scholarship at arguably the top program on the west coast. But here we were; two guys from two different ends of the spectrum with so little in common but also brought together by this game of basketball. And there it was our chance on Sunday March 22nd to do the impossible.

I always said at the end of the day when a team does something remarkable everybody gets remembered, whether you're the All-American who's getting ready to turn pro, or that guy at the end of the bench who waves the towel and plays for 1 minute. Teams need guys like that, at any level. The talk that Jordan and I had would last for several hours and then finally we both got some sleep. A part of me was surprised he gave me the time of day because this was a guy who typically didn't like conversing with anyone unless he wanted something from me or wanted me to do something.

So much was on the line when we were going to play in the second round of the NCAA Tournament. I still couldn't believe we were playing for a chance to go to the sweet sixteen. The mood, along with everyone's face had shifted from happy to business like from the moment we got on the bus to the moment we got into the arena. I kept thinking of that saying "When preparation meets opportunity that is luck". I didn't think we needed luck to go out there and win, we needed to do the things we were taught since the season started, put it all together, provide the effort and get the outcome we knew we could get.

The game was a route, they tried to make a comeback and it looked like it was going to be interesting for a few moments but our team was too determined to make it to a place where everyone thought we were prohibited from. As the clock was winding down slowly, the crowd of fans, who were wearing red and scattered throughout the different sections of the arena, rose to their feet and started chanting "Sweet-16" repeatedly.

When the clock finally got low enough for us to soak it in it felt like something I had never felt before. My senior day was a nice moment; but advancing to the sweet sixteen was phenomenal, almost ground breaking in a sense. The row of people on our bench, starting with our interim head coach and staff began to rose, and trickled all the way down to the end where I was sitting on the edge and then stood up. It was all the support we needed for those forty minutes.

The buzzer sounded, our trainer Justin looked at me and smiled and extended his hand; congratulating a few of the other guys on the bench, along with myself on making it to the sweet sixteen. I looked at the crowd, started waiving my arms up and down, back and forth, and tried to keep them on their feet for as long as I could. We shook hands with the opponent; they gave us a good challenge, which we overcame. It was a pretty special and unique scene; like when the tortoise beat the hare and proved to everyone that the hare could keep up.

The locker room scene was crazy to say the least. Guys were hugging each other and on the verge of crying. A team that was once demoralized found out about ourselves and we realized that we could overcome any type of adversity thrown our way. It was unexplainable to say how we were feeling. Even the guys on the bench like me had so much emotion it was crazy. I just couldn't believe what was actually going on.

Coach Pennell began to talk to us and he looked at all of us and put his hands up and said "Gentlemen, welcome to the sweet sixteen." He had this huge smile on his face along with Coach Dunlap and Coach Geary. They deserved so much credit for being able to go through the year and deal with everything the way they did. They all handled it with nothing but class and it filtered down to all of us. Our backs were against the wall from day one of the season and we responded by journeying ourselves to the sweet sixteen. All of us had become proof that if a group of guys stick together during tough times in the trenches there's a light at the end of the tunnel.

When we were at the airport everyone was literally staring at us when we walked in. Some of our fans were there and there were just college basketball fans there in general. The whole scenery was wonderful. I don't think any of us slept on the plane ride home and the reason was because we couldn't. We were still on such a high from the two tournament games and now we were in the sweet sixteen. That five hour plane ride from Miami felt more like an hour plane ride. Everyone was laughing with each other and just looking forward for what was to come in the next few days. This was the most unusual group of guys to make something happen, that's where the irony came in; the whole year the team, like myself, had been busy settling for mediocrity and all we needed was a little push from our coaches to be extraordinary.

As we got off the plane and headed into the airport the media was there along with some fans and they greeted us with open arms. It was pretty cool to see a lot of people there just there for us considering the season we had and the adversity we had to face all year long. School was the next day and that was unreal to say the least. I walked into my class and students were clapping and even my professor was smiling asking me questions about the sweet 16. It was like we had earned the respect of the entire university because we were a resilient group and we kept pushing and plowing our way into the tournament and now into the sweet sixteen. The Daily Wildcat headline read "Sweet (16) Dreams." Our team had defined the words "March Madness" and made people stand up and take notice.

We were the talk of the town, for a few more days anyway. We had been the talk of the town all year but I felt like we finally had the respect of everyone, including all the people who were doubting us and saying we weren't capable of making a tournament run, let alone even making the tournament.

Here we were; preparing ourselves for the biggest game of our lives. Everyone was anxious to get to practice and start up again. The only problem was our practices leading up to Indianapolis were horrible. Our scout team was making our starting group look bad; if our main guys couldn't beat a scout team with two walk-ons then we didn't belong to get to the sweet sixteen.

At one point it got so bad that Coach Dunlap put us all on the line and ran us for about ten minutes which was later followed by wall-sits and extra conditioning. We had to pick it up if we were going to have any shot against Louisville. There was "kool-aid" being put in front of us by outsiders and third party influences, who had suddenly hopped back onto the band wagon and it was our job as a team not to drink it.

The only good thing was that the morale of the team was still high and positive and even though our practices were not what they should've been our morale was, and we could use that to channel that in the right direction. The last practice we had before we got on the plane to Indianapolis was actually pretty good. Guys were getting after it and playing hard which was a step in the right direction. We did a lot of shooting drills and position work before we left. The purpose was for everyone to get a great work out and get as many reps in as possible.

The practice was only an hour and thirty minutes at the most but it was an intense hour. From the shooting to the scrimmage everyone had to be on point and alert to what was going on. After the practice was over we still had about four hours or so before we had to go to the airport and get on the plane so we all stayed around to get some extra shots up and get ready. Coach Pennell brought us in and told us how great of an opportunity we had coming up and to take advantage of it. Pennell, along with the rest of the coaches was going to prepare us as well as they could, trying to make a statement to everyone who doubted us, from our own fans to our own administration, but once those bright lights shined, only we could take it from there.

Everything we had worked for was going to be put to the test; all the times we didn't want to have those early practices or extra shooting sessions. All of it was for a purpose come this time of year; our coaches harped on the fact that our season wasn't a sprint but it was a marathon. We were at the tail end of the marathon and somehow we were among college basketball's elite, surviving with the fittest and finding our place in the trenches.

When we were in Miami I only packed enough clothes in my duffle bag for one game; when my teammates found out they were upset. I told them my reason for doing this was motivation; I wanted the guys to be motivated and do what everyone thought we were incapable of all year long. This time around I packed extra clothes in my duffle bag, hoping that we could use a lifeline and advance to the next round of the tournament.

During the plane ride I kept thinking about the "what ifs", if we were to win and have a chance to get to the final four, it might have been one of the best stories in sports for years to come. Lose and my career, along with a few other guys on the team would be over and the reconstruction of a program would officially begin.

We could watch as much film as we did and practice as much as we wanted and have all the walk-through's and extra shooting sessions but at the end of the day we had to go out to the arena, put on our war paint and win the battle. The arena we were playing in was enormous; so many seats that needed to be filled up by various fans from all over the place. Looking around I felt like we were a bunch of David's going up against a big Goliath who had no intentions of taking it easy on the remaining darlings of the tournament.

The court was elevated, making it look like a Broadway setting; I took the court and looked up at those bright lights; my voice would echo even though it was mono toned, the big stage we had played on became a bigger stage.

A lot of the nervousness we had felt in the first and second round of the tournament had left our bodies, I still felt something in mine; part of that was because I was a senior and this was do or die for me. This team was slowly but surely coming closer together and heating up at the right time which was fantastic but scary at the same time. I kept telling my parents that other teams were scared of us because we had that prized momentum on our side and we just had to carry it over to the game.

We had a regular full contact practice before our open public practice at this local college out in Indianapolis. This was that type of practice that was hard for some of the guys to get fired up for because our bodies were a little jet lag; guys were starting to get tired both physically and mentally. But it was one of those teaching practices that needed to be done because we needed to fine tune some things before we got out there Friday night. Everyone was on point for the most part. Our scout team was competing with the starters for as long as it took.

I remember at the end of the practice we played some shooting games for about fifteen to twenty minutes. At first my attitude was like "why?" Why would we be joking around and playing shooting games two days before the biggest game of our lives? There was a method that Coach Pennell had. He wanted us to be loose and relax our minds and not be so tight while we were up here, given the way the season had unfolded I didn't question his thinking, if I were in his position I probably would've done the same thing with our group of guys.

I noticed that when the stage got bigger and the stakes became higher with our group, individuality went out the window and that word "Team" started to become our savior; I could never tell what my teammates were thinking but I'm sure they reflected on their experience like I did, to a certain degree. You come this far and you can't help but reflect and cherish the time you have as a group because after that buzzer sounds one team would advance and one team would go home.

We had our group of fans that game out to support us, parents were there as well as fans from all over. Our turnout wasn't nearly as big as Louisville's because they were the overall number 1 seed in the tournament so they played their games closest to home and Louisville wasn't that far off from Indianapolis. As we took the court and started warming up we heard a mixture of boo's and applauses.

There were still those people that didn't give us any respect. None of us paid any attention to it, all we did was just laugh and continue to have our practice. The place was so big it was hard to pay attention to everything at one time, especially when there were so many cameras and media looking at you for that particular hour when we were on the court.

Back at the hotel we had a lot of downtime, it was one of the few times when I didn't do homework on the road, instead I just enjoyed the time I had. I was listening to the song "I can" by Nas and I closed my eyes and envisioned everything that I had gone through; the times when I felt like I wasn't going to make it, the times when I thought I wasn't good enough to play at the division one level, and then all the great memories I had leading up to where I currently was at.

It's funny because when I started this journey as a walk-on out back in 2005 I felt like at any given point and time I could get cut from the team or they could always just tell me to go home and that they didn't need me anymore. And I know it sounds crazy but I always had that fear in the back of my mind and I think that's what drove me to develop a work ethic and work just as hard as some of the starter without getting playing time or all the accolades they had received. But it really helped mold me into a better person.

If I hadn't gone through some of those rough times I went through when I was a freshman then I probably wouldn't have made it as a senior. And I fast forward 3 years later and here I am as a senior playing in the biggest game of my life. I never thought I would be doing this when I was in high school but its funny how a journey works out when you stick with it.

Right before I went to sleep Jordan and I were talking and we just looked at each other and thought about the game and how much it meant, for both of us. I was hoping and praying that we would be the team to dominate Louisville and make them look bad on national television. That was my vision, I played that scene in my mind 100 times of us advancing and shocking the world like a true underdog would.

Friday morning came way too quick; I remember when I woke up I fell off my bed because I thought I was going to be late for our team breakfast. The mood was relaxed, not too relaxed but business like relaxed. We had everything laid out in front of us for our game. We had the Film, stats, tendencies, breakdowns, the whole nine yards. The question on everyone's minds now was if we could get this done. There was no doubt in my mind that we could, crap I just wanted the game to come.

We had one last rehearsal at the Lucas Oil Stadium; our shoot-around was pretty intense like they had been all year long and it was our last chance to fine tune some things before the lights cameras came down.

When I was back in the hotel room after our pre-game meal I was looking at my Jersey one last time before I put it on. Just thinking about what it meant to be in this game and how we turned around our season. We all had a part in helping out someway and now we were 2 hours away from tip-off.

Lucas Oil Stadium looked a lot different with 73 thousand fans in there, most of them were Louisville fans but still, the atmosphere was nuts. We went out to warm up and it was pretty quiet except for this one little area right across from our bench because that's where all of our fans were at. They were screaming as loud as they could but I couldn't really hear them once Louisville took the court.

As soon as they came out the whole arena erupted and that sea of red just got bigger and bigger. I tried to think of that red as Arizona red instead of Louisville red. It was a little intimidating, virtually a home game for Louisville but they were the overall number 1 seed in the tournament.

When they announced the starters and we huddled up as a team I had one last thing to tell the guys before they got out there. I said that nobody expected us to be here except us; no one thought we could make this run and on one thought we had chance. I said there was no tomorrow for this team and we had to play like that. It was awesome jumping around with those guys and firing everyone up, I loved doing that. Coach Pennell was firing us up in our team huddle and telling us to get after it. Now was our time to get out there and make it happen.

The best story would've been for us to jump on them right away and never look back as we made our way to the next round of the tournament; but we were in for a very long night. When that ball went up and Jordan lost the tip they immediately came down and hit a jump shot. Turned out Louisville was just getting started and we were in for a long, long night. They jumped out to a 24-15 lead and never looked back. Not once did we have the lead in that game and it started to become ugly real quick. For whatever reason we just didn't seem to be in sync with each other; that's what it looked like from my view and Louisville was capitalizing on all of our mistakes.

I couldn't believe what I was seeing, our small group of fans had become so quiet and the Lucas Oil Stadium was roaring with Louisville cheers coming from every direction.

Coach Dunlap kept telling us to stick with it and emphasized how we needed to be there for our teammates as he had done throughout the year. The bench was part of the glue that held the team together especially on the road where it's a hostile environment.

We went into the locker room with our heads somewhat down and out but the crazy thing was that there was still another half of basketball left to be played. When Coach Pennell came into the locker room he looked at all of us; right in our eyes and told us to keep fighting and not let up. There was no way we could get back in the game if we gave up, we had to give a hundred and ten percent effort and play with the resiliency we had played with the first two games of the tournament and throughout most of the year.

I kept looking around at guy's faces in the locker room, everybody looked dejected, almost like we wanted to go home and move on. I think it was more shock than anything else. To come out and challenge a team as deep as Louisville we really had to be on top of our game and if the truth be told we came out extremely lethargic. I felt like guys could kind of sense the end was near.

Almost like they wanted to get back out there but no one wanted the embarrassment to continue but we really had no choice and there was no way we could go out like we were quitters. The way that game went was almost like being in a fight with no way of coming back to defend yourself, I felt bad because I was on the bench the whole time, watching my teammates give up shot after shot as the clock continued to wind down. As the game progressed, the bench, including me, became silent, almost voiceless. There was nothing I could've said or the coaches could've said that would've changed the game.

The lead kept growing and growing but with about a minute and a half left Coach Pennell called me to sub into the game. I was so fired up when I went in because we were down so much and all I could see in front of my face was that lead that had almost become 40 points. When I checked into the game I knew I was going to get a chance to shoot or do something because they had backed off of their pressure defense and it was pretty late in the game for both teams. I had a steal off of one of their guards and ironically, I scored the last basket for our team during our tournament run. It was a "moral basket" in a sense because we were already defeated; we just had to find our way home.

Towards the end of the game one of Louisville's players was shooting a free throw and I leaned down to talk to one of their guards. I told the guard I was standing next to that I thought they had a great chance to beat North Carolina and win the National Championship and how I'd never seen a team as deep as theirs before. I thought he was going to say thank you but his response was something that stuck out vividly in my mind and I'll always remember what he said. He looked at me and said "you guys suck."

It was unfortunate to end the sweet sixteen the way that we did; when the buzzer sounded our fans stood up and cheered which was soon put to silence when the Louisville fans stood up and cheered for their team. We walked off the court as a unit; I had tears running down my face because the journey had finally ended. I walked off the hardwood wearing an Arizona basketball jersey for the last time, standing next to Chase, who also had a dejected look on his face.

At the other end of the hallway I could hear the Louisville fans cheering and saying things repeatedly, while at our end silence was at a premium and words couldn't describe the emotions we felt. The trenches we were journeying through had finally opened up and the battle was over. As a team, we lost that particular battle, but if our season was a war, we proved that we won, dealing with the ultimate adversity the way we did, bonding as a group together and coming out night after night and leaving emotion, effort, and hard work out on the floor.

We defied the odds and that's how everyone would remember the 2008-09 Arizona Basketball season. It was bittersweet, a great feel good story for years to come. A group of guys who were given little, if any respect, with their backs against the wall the whole season with nothing to lose and everything to gain showed what it means to have heart, courage, and resilience.

We were guided by a coaching staff that could've bailed on us when the tough got going but stuck together and came to our rescue from the very beginning. That was the way I remembered it. Of course there were obstacles along the journey; that was a given, everyone knew it was going to happen, but we showed a lot of people what we were made of and that's something absolutely nobody can take away from us.

The silence was continuous; nobody wanted to talk, nor did any of us know what to say, all I could hear were tears hitting the floor and the thoughts and reflections in my mind of a four year journey that ended right in front of me, filled with irony and memories.

Coach Pennell began to talk to us. His eyes were watery from the start; as were mine. I knew that once he cried, the emotion would be felt by all of us slowly, because of the way the year had gone, we were on an emotional rollercoaster for a while and the ride had finally ended. He told us how proud he was of us and we had nothing to be ashamed of. He told us that he'll always remember this team for the rest of his life because we never gave up or gave in. We stuck together and we were there for each other and that's the true meaning of a team. He went on to thank all of us as well as the other coaches for an outstanding season and then we brought it in one last time.

When Coach Pennell finished his speech, the administration walked in and our athletic director thanked all of us, praising us for sticking the season out and representing the school in a positive fashion. After the administration made their rounds, they walked out, like they had on us from the beginning, and we were left in a Locke room with our original family we had started out with from the beginning of the season. Coach Pennell called us in for one last team huddle.

I loved those team huddles because at least at one point for everyone even if certain guys didn't get along it brought everyone together for a few seconds. We said the word "family" as we had been doing since I was a freshman. We all went around hugging each other, crying, and telling each other how much we cared for one another. Nobody knew what was going to happen next.

Of course there always guys that were pursing professional careers but outside of a select few, nobody knew what the next phase had in store for anyone. That's the beauty of the basketball season; it brings everyone together for a few months out of the year and it's always something you can look back on fifteen years from now with memories. I sure had a lot to look back on from the last four years.

My body was numb, my mind was clouded with memories and thoughts, my eyes were red, and it didn't really even hit me yet that four years had flown by all too fast. But it was over, and we had cemented our legacy by making a run in the NCAA Tournament. It's something that all teams dream of doing and we were closer than most. Losing in the sweet sixteen was not a national championship, but it was a positive way to end after everything we'd gone through.

I got on the bus and turned on my phone and I had over fifty messages and about five voicemails. Friends and family said how proud they were of me and how far I'd come. Words couldn't explain the emotion that I was feeling sitting with all those guys on the team bus for the last time. Zane, Jordan and I grabbed dinner that night and for two hours we were praised by Louisville fans as well as other college basketball fans in there; saying how proud they were and what a resilient group of athletes we were.

All I could do was smile and say thank you. And a few people came up to me and said I had a nice three point shot at the end. That's what it was for me, the end. I kept thinking if we had beaten Louisville and had a chance at the final four we could've gone down as one of the most loved teams in the school's history; but I knew what we had accomplished would have people talking for the next few years.

We were greeted back in Tucson by the local media as well as the fans and people were clapping and smiling at all of us. That was the moment when I knew that we had finally gained the respect of everyone, not just our friends or our family but everyone. Realistically nobody gave us a chance and we proved a lot of people wrong with the way we played during certain points throughout the year.

When I went to class this time after we lost everybody I my class looked at me and smiled or gave me the nod like they were proud of us. The feedback was nothing but respect. Of course there were a few people that said we should've played better but there are people like that everywhere. The whole university had grown to respect us, it only took us the whole season but it was well worth it. All I had to look forward to now was graduation and what the next phase of my life had in store for me.

It was different not having to wake up early anymore for early lifting or shooting or anything like that. I finally got to relax for a few days and enjoy my last few months as a student instead of a student-athlete. My parents occasionally checked in on me, seeing how I was holding up since everything was over. They told me to finish out the year strong and focus on school as much as I could.

Arizona as an institution and a program had given me a unique opportunity for four years and I had many opportunities being a walk-on. They had to transition into hiring a new coach and bring back the stability that the program was missing the last two years. A part of me was hoping that Coach Pennell would get the head coaching job, the guy showed all year he cared about us and that goes a long way in athletics.

We lobbied for the guy, along with the rest of the staff but before we could plea our case to the administration, Coach Dunlap took an assistant coaching job at Oregon. Dunlap was like a professor with his words and the way he taught us offensive and defense. His mind worked on the clock and to him the practice floor was like a laboratory; no one could see what we were doing in there and we were like scientists hard at work. Opportunities were opening up for the coaches because of the season we wound up having.

Coach Pennell had taken the head coaching job at Grand Canyon State University in Phoenix. Reggie had landed an assistant coaching job at Southern Methodist University in Texas. These schools were getting three great people to help point them in better directions. I was sad to see all of them leave; we had built a special bond with each other throughout the year but that's how fast the season goes by.

Everything was happening all at once and I hardly saw my teammates the last couple weeks of school, everyone was starting to go their separate ways. Jordan and Chase were preparing themselves for the NBA draft; everyone knew they were going to get drafted, I mean they carried us all year long and they played like pros game in and game out. I saw my other teammates here and there whether it was in the weight room or playing pickup games with them at our recreational center.

Everything seemed to work itself out for a lot of us; we rallied around each other and had a unique season. Our coaching staff was rewarded for the way they took care of us and for the job they did the whole year. The program hired a great coach who was ready to take the reins and move forward and build his own legacy, and the next phase of the life of a walk-on was waiting.

My main focus was graduation; it was about seven weeks away and I had to really focus on that because as much as I loved playing and doing all of that graduation was the top priority because let's face it; without a degree you're limited to a certain degree. I carried over the work ethic I had from basketball and applied it to the remaining weeks of school and I graduated with over a 3.0 grade point average. That meant a lot to me, almost as much as any three point shot I hit in a game because to graduate is one thing but to graduate with over a 3.0 meant even more. I loved going to school and learning new things and applying education and what I've learned to everyday life.

I remember Coach Dunlap telling me how important it was to graduate because of what it meant when you're an athlete and you get your degree. It shows how well you can balance things that are thrown your way and says a lot about who you are as a person. A lot of people underestimate athletes when they try and graduate or get their degrees but I'm happy to say I was able to do it in four years even with my other job being a basketball player. Graduation finally marked the end of college, it was time to look ahead and move forward to whatever was in store for me. Coach Dunlap was right, there's a moment in time that stops, it comes when you're accepting your diploma and all the kudos for what you have done in college and you're taking a step forward into the next phase of your life. You ask yourself "What's next?"

When the season was over and the program was transitioning, I'd still go back to our arena, the McKale Center late at night, and stand on the circle at half court that had Coach Olson's name on it, as well as our locker room. A few times I'd bring a ball with me, but usually I would just stand there, close my eyes, and reflect on the unique four year journey I embarked on as a walk-on.

The experience circled back to me while I was standing at half court and it was time to answer those two questions I had written at the beginning of my senior year. I had constant reminders from my father about what I learned from this experience as a walk-on and I proposed the question to myself about how I wanted to be remembered when the experience was all said and done.

There was a whole laundry list in terms of what I learned from the experience of a walk-on. When it was all said and done, I learned that Coach Olson, the man that turned my window of opportunity into a reality and a dream come true, was right; if you embrace an opportunity that comes knocking on your doorstep then the opportunity will embrace you back in some way, sometimes in many ways that aren't expected. I learned what it was like to not only face the best competition in the country on a daily basis, but challenge them as well, doing everything from getting dunked on by All-Americans to getting under their skin in practice.

I had to earn everything in four years, from my stripes to the food at our team meals, to the privilege of getting my ankles taped before games. I also had to earn the respect I got from my teammates, coaches, and everyone else in-between and that was one of the many challenges that were laid out in front of me since I was a freshman. Accepting the fact that nothing was going to be handed to me made me work that much harder, and my reward was a large sized seat that was outside the lines that I got to be a part of during the waning moments of a game.

My teammates were like my brothers; every workout, team activity, practice and game we harped on the word "family". When I started out saying the word I felt like I was distant family, I had to earn my right to be part of the immediate family which eventually happened when I became a senior. In a sense, certain teammates and individuals did me the best favor and helped me out with the experience in some way, challenging my will as much as they could, whether it was verbally belittling me, telling me I didn't belong, public humiliation in front of my friends, or even going as far as physically hitting me to prove a point and showing why college basketball for a walk-on, is equivalent to survival of the fittest.

I learned that fear, like limits, are just an illusion, a person can do anything given the will, the determination, and the focus displayed on hand; and if a fire burns strong enough in someone that is just perceived as "mediocre", then an impact can be made in some way, even though it goes unnoticed by those on the outside looking in.

Quitting the team was never a real option for me; towards the end of my junior year I salt and peppered with the idea but never acted on it; it was a quick exit, a chance to run away from the everyday challenge of trying to compartmentalize the task of being a student-athlete and a dead end that would've led me to question myself as well as live in regret for the rest of my life, and it would've given me a permanent void that would've never been filled and would've had

151

me doubting myself; but I never doubted I could keep up with those guys, I realized that I always could, it was equivalent to gravity, I just needed a little push.

The empty weight room, the end of the bench, and an empty arena filled with garbage, bugs and rodents often became my home away from home, it became my sanctuary, a place where I found what I sought out to look for, perfect my routine that became invaluable, hone my skills, and realize that I was more than a guy that rarely played and had the best seat in the house.

I found peace and quiet in the arena on the nights when I heard nothing but the lights buzzing, continuous squeaking of my sneakers, and saw empty seats with nobody cheering for me. That was the beautiful part about the whole experience, the motivation came from within, not from a coach or teammate or friend, but from me, a guy that nobody expected to be motivated because I was so happy to be on the team.

I felt the adrenaline and experienced on numerous occasions, firsthand what it was like to have a group of students sitting there and rally around a guy sitting several feet across from them in a gym filled up with a crop of fans of all ages; they felt what I felt, the undeniable urge to get into the game and help contribute to the team in some fashion. That's what it always was in a nutshell, a guy sitting and waiting, patiently, who always wanted to contribute in some way so people would take into account the hard work that goes into not playing but having what it takes to be on the tam.

I never felt sorry for myself sitting on that bench, or standing on that sideline in practices, nor did I ever doubt my purpose as a walk-on. If anything, I felt excited to be a member of an elite fraternity that was known as college basketball. Every year, thousands of kids across the nation lace up limited edition team sneakers, put on a pair of shorts that are only issued for them, and wear a jersey with the name on the front that will always outweigh the name on the back. I was blessed to say that I was one of those kids and cherished every moment of it because every team needs a guy to hold down the team GPA, go to community service events when no one else wants to, and wave a towel at the end of the bench with prayers and high hopes of getting in at the end of the game. Having a role on the team is like having a job; if you're not doing it right, they can bring someone in who will.

Looking over my shoulder for four years and having the fear of getting cut or told my services were no longer needed started at as self doubt but later turned into self motivation. That's what a walk-on really is; a guy who's not supposed to be on the team but finds a niche of some sort and tries to stick the journey out in any way possible.

It's someone who finds motivation from within and uses all the energy possible to gain respect in the end, some notice it and others don't care for it, that's the beauty of those two words "walk-on". There's a permanent asterisk next to someone's name which signifies those two words; it forces regular people on the outside to raise their eyebrows and propose questions like "What does that mean? Did you ever play? What are your teammates like?"

Those two words, along with the journey, take mediocre people for a roller coaster of a ride, jerk people's emotions side to side and upside down. But when that roller coaster comes to a stop, you can look yourself in the mirror with confidence and pride and say you were able to compete with the top competition in the nation, and it didn't matter the time of day, what emotions were going through your head, or what other people thought, what mattered was that there was always a light at the end of the tunnel, I just had to find a way out.

I found out in the end it is definitely worth it; that was the only question I ever asked myself going forward as I prepared for every season. Is it worth it? But in the end, after proposing that question numerous times I found out it always was, because that's what a journey is; it's a progress from one stage to the next. And after you progress from that stage, you come out a better person.

The other question I put forward was when I started my senior year and I asked myself "How do you want to be remembered?" It's beyond easy for guys that actually play to mold their own legacy as oppose to a guy that limps onto the scene who's not supposed to be there, sits on a bench and hopes for a shot at the end of the games. Every year players come, go, and then get forgotten; that made my job harder to try and figure out the way people would remember a walk-on.

Looking back and reflecting, I wouldn't have traded anything in this experience for what the "main players" had. I never had to worry about having a bad game, missing the game winning shot, watching extra hours of film, and everything else that goes along with being a starter on a college basketball team. I had to worry about being early for classes, conducting study sessions for my teammates, raising the team GPA, catering to certain teammates and then trying to get the best out of them as much as I could in a two hour practice, cheer for them as loud as I could, check into a game with minimal time remaining, launch a jump-shot from wherever I could, and pray to God that it goes in so the crowd would still chant my name and help me out. I had to worry about this all while dealing with the simple fear that scratches the surface in every athletes head: Getting cut.

I wanted to be remembered as a guy who pushed players in practices and helped them reach their fullest potential as they moved forward; because they certainly helped me reach mine, even though fans never got to see a glimpse of what I could really do. Towards the end of my senior year, one of my teammates called me the greater good of the team; his reasoning was because of everything I offered to do help the team and my teammates out, whether it was rebounding for them after practice, doing homework for them, or simply just being there so they could vent to me about the pressures they felt as elite college basketball players.

A student told me before I graduated, and not in a bad way, that because of my role on the team as a walk-on, I became the link between the regular students on campus and the basketball team. My teammates, often regarded as the "Big men on campus", were untouchable, and unapproachable in a sense; everyone rooted for them to succeed on the court because when they played well, they made our team successful; but they were scared of them when they saw them up and close, whether it was in a social setting or in a classroom. Then I came along; a six foot five inch walk-on, a lanky individual, who had a jump-shot, a baby-faced smile, and a team first attitude that certain people fed off of.

Whether I liked it or not, I was someone that people could relate to, due to the fact that those two words "Walk-On", personified mediocrity, regularity, and ordinary, even though being a member of an elite college basketball team required me to be extraordinary in everything I did, both on and off the court. Students felt comfortable around somebody they could relate to, often picturing themselves doing what I did and pondering the "What ifs", just like I would do. It may have looked easy to sit on the bench for four years but it certainly was not. When push comes to shove, competitive juices, mixed with adrenaline and skill good enough to keep up, are begging to get on that court for more than a minute and some change. Guys back home, from high school and my gym, used to tell me that I was a guy who was connected to a bench I never got off of; in a way they were right, but that bench was also connected to me, in more ways than one.

I always knew there were people who rooted for me to fail, from certain teammates whose skin I got underneath on a daily basis, to students that questioned why I was on the team, to the fans that were playing tug-a-war, going back and forth on our bandwagon and leaving our arena as I checked in. It's easy to root against a guy who doesn't play because he's not supposed to be there in the first place; to all the outsiders, he caught a break, it was hard to accept the fact that someone of mediocre ability could often find success because eventually the length of the journey and obstacles would eventually take a toll and show me the way out.

Moving forward, when fans, and people think of the word "Walk-On", I know there will always be groups of individuals in every place that don't care or have no interest to disclose an opinion because it's not worth their breath, time, or energy, which is fine, that's how the system of athletics goes; everyone appreciates the guys who bring home the stats and reel in the highlights.

The guy that doesn't play expects the unexpected and I learned that first hand in everything I did through four unique years of college basketball. I hope people would no longer think of a walk-on as an athlete that is often looked at as the team's whipping boy, that guy that rarely sees playing time or doesn't receive any glory for all the unnoticed work that is being put in on a daily basis when absolutely no one is watching. After reading my story about my journey as a college basketball player; when people hear those two words "Walk-on", I hope they will stop, think and then say to themselves, "Yeah, a walk-on, he was part of that glue, he helped hold the team together".

Special Thanks to...

My famiy, Mom, Dad, Derek, Grandma Ann
Mitch Garcia
Lute Olson
Jim Rosborough
Josh Pastner
Miles Simon
Russ Pennell
Mike Dunlap
Reggie Geary
Dewie Pennell
Kevin O'Neill
Chase Budinger
Fendi Onobun
Nic Wise
DJ Shumpert
Bret Brielmaier
Daniel Dillon
Kirk Walters
Mohamed Tangara
Mustafa Shakur
Ivan Radenovic'
Jawann MaClellan
Alex Jacobson
Hassan Adams
Chris Rodgers
Jerryd Bayless
Jamelle Horne
Zane Johnson
Kyle Fogg
Brendon Lavender
Isaiah Fox
JP Prince
Garland Judkins
Jesus Verdejo

Jordan Hill
Lucas Spencer
Matt Brase
Jesse Mermuys
Justin Kokoskie
Ryan "Ryno" Hansen
Joseph Blair
President Robert Shelton and President Peter Likins
Jim Livengood
Rocky LaRose
Bill Morgan
Joe Jensen
Jamal Boddie
Jake Jackson
Jeff Feld
Ben Tucker
Paul Torres
Ryan Hennick
Adam Cohan
Sean Hennick
Joe Jensen
Greg Rosbourough
Danny Corrales
Adam Raczynski
Alan Peterson
Jim Hawkins
Tim Phenning
Benny Conger
Lisa Napolean
Becky Bell
Jennifer Mewes
Mike Mead
Andy Salgado
Phoebe Chalk
Jim Krumpos
Neil Rampe
Cory Edmond

Mark Hill
Steven Dilustro
Lisa Watson
Marysol Quiroz
Jim Story
John Ash
Jason Ranne
Fil Torres
Jason Stuart
Patty Otta
Wendell Neal
Randy Cohan
Dr. David Millward
Dr. Scott Goldman
Dr. Don Porter
Donna Swaim
Russ Andeloro
Richard Paige
Brian Jeffries
Bryan Roy
OJ Lipscomb
Monica Armenta
Jill Hall
Bryan Odom
Dan Tobias
Frank Busch
Andy Lopez
Dave Rubio
Dana Kaner
Jessica Manos
Lindsay Felix
Nathalie Dube
Bruce Pasco
Steve Rivera
Patrick Finley
Brandon Nash
Roger Haines

Jack Murphy
Dylan Rigdon
Blake Arnett
Peter Leav
Kent Rockwell
Keith Wilkinson
Drew Terry
Ojay Lipscomb
Mark White
Mark Campbell
Alex Holmes
Alex Millinovic
Jason Jepson
Anthony Earley
Micah Whittman
Genai Kerr
Teague Shen
Geoff Meyers
Greg Bloom
Jim Mitchell
Ryan Moore
Cory Kelly
Walter Almenderez
Ray Ethridge
Craig Bennett
Jeff Koga
"The lakeshore legends"
The Zona' Zoo student section
And to all the fans that made my experience as a walk-on wonderful
for 4 years

CPSIA information can be obtained at www.ICGtesting.com
Printed in the USA
BVOW040943301111

276849BV00002B/25/P